PREMIUM ESSAY

ON

PROPHETIC SYMBOLS.

THE PREMIUM ESSAY

ON

THE CHARACTERISTICS AND LAWS

OF

PROPHETIC SYMBOLS.

BY

THE REV. EDWARD WINTHROP, A. M.,

RECTOR OF ST. PAUL'S CHURCH, NORWALK, OHIO

There is a God in heaven that revealeth secrets, and maketh known . . . what shall be in the latter days.—*Dan.* ii. 28.

THIRD EDITION.

NEW YORK:

PUBLISHED BY FRANKLIN KNIGHT,

138 NASSAU STREET.

1855.

CONTENTS.

Page

CHAPTER IV.

CHAPTER V.

CHAPTER VI.

CHAPTER VII.

CHAPTER VIII.

CHAPTER IX.

CHAPTER X.

CHAPTER XI.

RESULTS OF THESE LAWS.

Page

CHAPTER XII.

ANSWER TO OBJECTIONS AGAINST THE SEVENTH RESULT.

CHAPTER XIII.

RESULTS—(Continued.)

CHAPTER XIV.

PREFACE.

THE occasion and object of this Essay will be explained by the following Circular, issued in June, 1851:

"PREMIUMS OFFERED FOR THREE ESSAYS ON THE CHARACTERISTICS AND LAWS OF PROPHETIC SYMBOLS.

"*The views of the Characteristics and Laws of Prophetic Symbolization*, presented in the THEOLOGICAL AND LITERARY JOURNAL, have attracted the attention of many persons in different parts of the country, especially of those in the Sacred Office, excited curiosity and investigation, and induced the feeling that they are entitled to a careful consideration by the students of the Bible.

"It is known that a very considerable number have become satisfied of the accuracy of these laws, and deem it of great moment that they should be generally understood and adopted. Another class, who regard them with much interest, and find themselves at a loss how to confute them, or set aside the constructions to which they lead, nevertheless, hesitate to give them their full assent, and before they finally determine, desire to know what can be said against them by the advocates of other systems of interpretation. A third class reject them, not, so far as is known, on the ground of any direct evidence of their inaccuracy, but because the results to which they lead conflict with the views they have been accustomed to entertain of the administration God is hereafter to exercise over the world.

"A strong wish is felt, therefore, by many of these several classes, that the validity of these laws should be tried in some form that will enable inquirers generally, and especially such as have not leisure for a minute investigation, to decide more satisfactorily in respect to them; and for that purpose a fund has been subscribed to offer as premiums for three essays on the subject, that shall be deemed, by parties to be named as Adjudicators, the best entitled to them;—the point to be argued and proved being whether those Characteristics and Laws are, or are not, the true Characteristics and Laws of Prophetic Symbols; and the sum of Four Hundred Dollars to be awarded and paid to the Author of the Essay which most legitimately and effectively demonstrates the alternative he endeavors to establish; the sum of Two Hundred Dollars to the Author of the Essay the next in merit in that respect; and the sum of One Hundred Dollars to the Author of the Essay the third in rank in that relation; provided, that of those presented, three of them are of such character and merit as justly to be entitled to the premiums.

"The chief points to be discussed by the Essayists are the views presented in the JOURNAL, and other works of the Editor,* respecting—

I. THE NATURE AND OFFICE OF PROPHETIC SYMBOLS

* Mr. David N. Lord, of the city of New York.

II. THE MARKS BY WHICH THE SYMBOLIC PROPHECIES ARE DISTINGUISHABLE FROM THOSE OF WHICH LANGUAGE IS THE MEDIUM:

III. THE CLASSIFICATION OF THE SYMBOLS:

IV. THE PRINCIPLES ON WHICH THEY ARE EMPLOYED:

V. THEIR LAWS:

VI. WHETHER THE SYMBOLS THAT ARE INTERPRETED IN THE PROPHECIES ARE INTERPRETED BY THESE LAWS:

VII. WHETHER INTERPRETATIONS ARE GIVEN IN THE PROPHECIES OF ONE OR MORE OF EACH CLASS OF SYMBOLS:

VIII. WHETHER THESE INSPIRED INTERPRETATIONS ARE TO BE REGARDED AS A REVELATION OF THE PRINCIPLE ON WHICH SYMBOLS ARE EMPLOYED, AND THE LAWS BY WHICH THEY ARE FRAMED, REVEALED LAWS:

IX. THE RESULTS TO WHICH THEY LEAD,—WHETHER THEY OBVIATE DIFFICULTIES, REMOVE UNCERTAINTIES, SUPPLY IMPORTANT DEFECTS, GIVE CONSISTENCY AND CERTAINTY TO INTERPRETATION, AND LEAD TO A CLEAR AND DEMONSTRABLE EXPLICATION OF MANY SYMBOLS OF WHICH NO SATISFACTORY SOLUTION IS OBTAINED BY OTHER SYSTEMS OF CONSTRUCTION:

X. THE EASE WITH WHICH THEY MAY BE MASTERED AND MADE THE MEANS OF A LARGE AND USEFUL KNOWLEDGE OF THE PROPHECIES:

XI. THEIR CLAIMS TO THE CONSIDERATION OF MINISTERS OF THE SACRED WORD, AND OF CHRISTIANS GENERALLY.

"Writers are at liberty to select and arrange the order of

the points they may discuss to suit themselves; and it is expected that they will not merely state their opinions, but give their reasons also for the judgment which they express; and that those who reject the views advanced in the JOURNAL will state what they regard as the true Characteristics and Laws of Prophetic Symbols, and the considerations by which they believe them to be sustained.

"Men of ability and high standing will be selected as the Adjudicators, whose names will be duly announced.

"The Essays which obtain the awards are to be the property of the contributors to the Premium Fund, and to be published in the JOURNAL or otherwise, as they may deem expedient.

"The Manuscripts, with a note from the author, should be addressed to the Adjudicators, and sent (post paid) to Franklin Knight, Publisher of the THEOLOGICAL AND LITERARY JOURNAL, 140 Nassau street, New York, on or before the 1st of February, 1852.

"Many clergymen and other gentlemen have expressed a desire that this subject, which they regard as one of great interest and importance, may be thus carefully investigated and thoroughly discussed—among whom are the following:

"Rev. James S. Cannon, D.D., Rutgers College, N. J.; Rt. Rev. Charles P. M'Ilvaine, D.D., Ohio; Rev. Nathan Lord, D.D., Dartmouth College, N. H.; Rev. Leonard Woods, D.D., Mass.; Rev. John Forsyth, D.D., Princeton College, N. J.; Rev. Mark Hopkins, D.D., Williams College, Mass.; Rev. J. H. Thornwell, D.D., S. C.; Rt. Rev. J. P. K. Henshaw, D.D., R. I.; Rev. Willis Lord, D.D., Ohio; Rev. Leroy M. Lee, D.D., Va.; Rev. Edward N. Kirk, D.D., Mass.; Rev. William Thompson, D.D., Theol. Inst., Conn.;

Rev. Edward Hitchcock, D.D., Amherst College, Mass.; Rt. Rev. Alonzo Potter, D.D., Pa.; Rev. Robert Ryland, Richmond College, Va.; Rev. George Duffield, D.D., Mich.; Rev. Henry Gregory, D.D., N. Y.; Rev. John M. Krebs, D.D., N. Y.; Rev. Isaac Anderson, D.D., Tenn.; Rev. Richard Newton, D.D., Pa.; Rev. Edward Winthrop, Ohio; Rev. Charles K. Imbrie, N. J.; Rev. Thomas E. Peck, Md.; Rev. Randolph Campbell, Mass.; Rev. William B. Stevens, D.D., Pa.; Rev. L. H. Van Doren, N. J.; Rev. M. L. P. Thompson, D.D., N.Y.; Rev. Walter Clarke, D.D., Conn.; Rev. John Richards, D.D., N. H.; Rev. J. F. Halsey, N. J.; Rev. D. S. Miller, Pa.; Rev. Adam Empie, D.D., Va.; Rev. George Potts, D.D., N. Y.; Rev. John M. Macauley, N. Y.; Rev. William Ramsey, Pa.; Rev. Thomas V. Moore, D.D., Va.; Rev. William R. Williams, D.D., N. Y.; Rev. E. Dunlap Smith, D.D., N. Y.; Rev. W. W. Blauvelt, N. J.; Rev. J. T. Ward, Pa.; Hon. J. C. Hornblower, N. J.; Hon. Bellamy Storer, Ohio; Messrs. Benjamin Douglass, Henry Smith, James Donaldson, B. R. Winthrop, D. O. Calkins, Chester Driggs, N. Y."

New York, June 10th, 1851.

Such was the Circular. The Rt. Rev. Charles P. M'Ilvaine, D.D., D.C.L.; the Rev. Alexander T. M'Gill, D.D.; and the Rev. John Forsyth, Jr., D.D., consented to act as Adjudicators. The result is that but one premium has been awarded, and that to the writer of the following Essay.

The author has carefully discussed all the topics

proposed in the Circular; and in revising his work for the press, has endeavored to present the argument with clearness and condensation, to call the attention of the reader to the exact line of reasoning, to answer the main objections, and to bring out prominently some of the chief results of the laws here demonstrated. He indulges the hope that this Essay, on THE CHARACTERISTICS AND LAWS OF PROPHETIC SYMBOLS, will prove a useful contribution towards the settlement of right principles for the interpretation of the Word of God; and thus be the means of advancing the Redeemer's glory, confirming the faith of his people, and unfolding the revealed plan of the divine administration.

EDWARD WINTHROP.

NORWALK, OHIO, *November 11th*, 1853.

CHARACTERISTICS AND LAWS

OF

PROPHETIC SYMBOLS.

CHAPTER I.

INTRODUCTION.—Design of the present Essay—the Holy Scriptures, the paramount authority in this inquiry—mode of argument and line of discussion adopted by the author—NATURE AND OFFICE OF PROPHETIC SYMBOLS—they are not figures of speech—difference between symbols and metaphors—their representative import proved by various examples from the Scriptures—MARKS BY WHICH SYMBOLIC PROPHECIES ARE DISTINGUISHABLE FROM THOSE WHICH ARE VERBAL.

THE prophetic Scriptures reveal to us the purposes of God and the destinies of men; and hence, to demonstrate the true principles on which these Scriptures are to be interpreted, and to develop the consequences of their correct application, is to confer a lasting benefit on all who love the sacred oracles, and bow, with adoring acquiescence, to their infallible decisions.

It is our design, in the present essay, to exhibit the nature and office of prophetic symbols; to point out certain marks by which the symbolic are distinguishable from the verbal prophecies; to arrange the symbols in classes; to unfold the principle on which they are employed; to expound their laws; to show that the symbols interpreted in the prophecies are interpreted by these laws; that interpretations of one or more of each class of symbols are given in the prophecies; and that these inspired interpretations are to be regarded as a revelation of the principle applicable to all the symbols, and the laws by which they are framed revealed laws; to notice the results to which they lead, and the ease with which they may be mastered and made the means of a large and useful knowledge of the prophecies; and to present the claims which they have upon the attention both of ministers and people.

These are the topics to which the Circular* calls our attention. We shall examine them all, and discuss them thoroughly, but with as much brevity as justice to the subject will admit.

In traversing this wide field of inquiry, the Holy Scriptures must be the lamp by which our feet are to be guided; for it is only by walking

* See Preface, p. ix.

in the light of these divine oracles, that we shall be kept from going astray. We must resort not to the fancies of ancient soothsayers, or the speculations of modern rationalists, but to the Bible itself, in order to perceive the manner in which symbols are used, and to deduce the laws by which they are to be explained. A careful and accurate analysis of passages from the word of God is absolutely indispensable; and that will undeniably be the best and most powerful mode of reasoning, which, by the clearness of its statements and the simplicity of its proofs, carries conviction to the unbiassed mind. Luminous and consistent exposition, therefore, in which we compare Scripture with Scripture to show the true meaning of the inspired volume, and to exhibit *the principles of interpretation which those Scriptures themselves reveal*, is the kind of discussion most needed. Such will be the line of argument in this essay. Avoiding collateral issues, and confining ourselves, for the most part, to the main points in question, we shall endeavor to ascertain the real import of the symbols themselves, as well as of the language which describes them. We hope that our readers will study the work with attention, fairness, and candor; for on such a subject involving the most grave and momentous questions, it is only by divesting ourselves, as far as possible, of all perverting influences, and examining the evidence deliberately, impartially, and prayerfully—looking to the Spirit of God to guide us in our investigations—that we can arrive at the truth.

Let us then consider, in the first place, THE NATURE AND OFFICE OF PROPHETIC SYMBOLS.

The symbols are *not rhetorical images* employed by the prophets, that is, they are *not figures of speech:* but they are *representative agents and objects* (with their acts, effects, characteristics, conditions, and relations); and, unless naturally perceptible, they were in dream, or vision, made perceptible by the Almighty, who thus indicated what should come to pass at the time appointed: and hence a *metaphor* (which is *a mere mode of expression*) and a *symbol* (which is an *agent, object, act, effect*), though often confounded by writers on prophecy, are entirely distinct from each other.

Thus when the Psalmist says, "the Lord is . . . my high tower," Psl. xviii. 2, there is a *metaphor.* Jehovah, and no one else, is the subject of the affirmation. The *metaphor* is in the phrase *high tower:* and the *figure of speech* consists in predicating of the Deity that which, in the literal sense of the words, is incompatible with his nature, it being impossible that God who is a spirit, a living being, should be literally a wooden or stone building, a mere inanimate edifice, such as is called a tower. The meaning of the Psalmist obviously is, that as men resort to a tower for defence and security, so he trusted in the Lord for defence and security; and therefore on account of the attributes by which he is capable of affording protection, the qualities in which, in a certain relation, he resembles a strong building, Jehovah is figuratively denominated *a tower*, which literally he is not. Nor is the language in Psl. xviii. 2, descriptive of any scenic representation either naturally or in vision, so that neither Jehovah nor the tower is there used as a symbol.

On the other hand, when Daniel says that he saw a he-goat rushing violently against a ram and overthrowing him, Dan. viii. 5–7, the terms *ram* and *he-goat* are not used metaphorically but literally, and designate exactly what was seen in the vision, namely, a literal ram and a literal he-goat acting in the manner described: and those animals were *symbols*, that is, they were *agents representing*, according to the inspired interpretation, Dan. viii. 20, 21, opposing *kings*.

In the great image, Dan. ii., the great tree, Dan. iv., and the four ravenous beasts, Dan. vii.,* we have examples of symbols which were perceptible in *dreams*: in the prophet Isaiah, chap. xx., the prophet Ezekiel, chap. iv., and the high priest with the crowns, Zech. vi., we have examples of symbols which were perceptible *naturally*; and in the locusts, Rev. ix., the seven-headed and ten-horned beast, and the two-horned beast, Rev. xiii., and the woman supported by the beast, Rev. xvii., we have examples of symbols which were perceptible in *ecstatic visions*.

The office of the symbols, the representative agents, objects, acts, effects, &c., is to denote agents, objects, acts, effects, &c., of the same order or kind, or those which are of a different but nevertheless analogous order. In the *dreams and visions* of the Hebrew prophets, and so too when those prophets or other real men were employed *naturally* as representative agents, and so also in the *dreams* of Nebuchadnezzar respecting the great image and the great tree, an agent, when used as a symbol, always symbolizes an *agent* and *not an act or effect*, *not a*

* "Daniel had a *dream* and visions of his head *upon his bed*: then he wrote the *dream*." Dan. vii. 1.

principle or system, not an attribute, quality, or condition: an object upon which agency is exerted always represents an object upon which agency is exerted: and the symbolic acts, effects, characteristics, conditions, and relations foreshow corresponding acts, effects, characteristics, conditions, and relations of the things symbolized. And thus whenever future events are disclosed exclusively through the medium of prophetic symbols, it is by a species of scenic representation.

That such is the nature and office of prophetic symbols, the Scriptures furnish the most ample proof. Thus, in the eighth chapter of Daniel, to recur to an example already given, the Medo-Persian dynasty is represented by a ram which had two horns. "The ram which thou sawest having two horns are the kings of Media and Persia," verse 20. The prophet says, "I saw the ram pushing westward, and northward, and southward," verse 4. The ram was a symbolical or *representative agent*, and his action, in pushing successfully against the other beasts, foreshowed the analogous action of the Medo-Persian kings against other chiefs in the same directions. The term "*ram*," as we have stated, is not used metaphorically but literally: and the language here employed, Dan. viii. 4, is simply descriptive of a past event which the prophet had seen in a vision, to wit, the agency of the ram. Hence the prediction in this verse is not at all through the medium of the language, but entirely through that of the symbols. By a correct interpretation of the *language* we learn what the symbol was, and what it did. The symbol was a ram, and the ram was seen pushing with his horns against other beasts, so that they could not stand before him. When therefore we have explained only *the meaning of the words*, we have not given an exposition of the true import of the prophecy. We have merely shown *what had been perceived in the vision.* In order to give a full exposition of *the prophecy*, we must show also what is signified *by the symbol, and by the agency which it exerted.* So also in regard to the "*he-goat.*" The *language* is so plain that it requires no comment—it is nearly all literal—the verbs are all in the past tense, and the prophecy is clearly through the medium of the symbols. "And as I was considering, behold a he-goat came from the west, on the face of the whole earth, and touched not the ground; and the goat had a notable horn between his eyes. And he came to the ram that had two horns, which I had seen standing before the river, and ran unto him in the fury of his power. And I saw him come close unto the ram, and he was moved with choler against him, and smote the ram, and brake his two horns: and there was no power in the ram to stand before him, but he cast him down to the ground, and stamped upon him: and there was none that could deliver the ram out of his hand." Dan. viii. 5–7. From the twenty-first verse we learn what was symbolized by the he-goat—"the king of Grecia: and the great horn that is between his eyes is the first king." The ram had been explained in verse twentieth, as symbolizing "the kings of Media and Persia." The overthrow of the ram, therefore, by the he-goat indicated the analogous overthrow of the Medo-Persian dynasty, and was historically verified in the conquest of Darius by Alexander the Great. The inspired interpretation in this, as in all similar cases, is an interpretation of *the symbols* only, and *not of the language:* and this is decisive that the prediction is through the medium of the former, and not through that of the latter. In many of the prophecies there is no prediction whatever, unless it be through the medium of the symbols: as in those just cited, and in that of the last resurrection and the final judgment, Rev. xx. 12–15, where, with the exception of the clause in verse fourteenth—"*this is the second death*"—which is an inspired interpretation thrown in parenthetically, all *the words* are descriptive of something that was past, namely, the symbolic exhibition which had been seen by St. John, and which foreshowed a corresponding future reality. Hence the only way in which this and other passages of similar construction can foreshow the future is *through the medium of* THE SYMBOLS, THE REPRESENTATIVE AGENTS, OBJECTS, AND ACTS *which point to the future.* This is just as true when the symbol is of the same class, order, or species, with the thing symbolized, as it is when it is of a different but analogous order. Thus the vision in Rev. xx. 12–15, is truly symbolic or representative in its import. The unholy raised from death, as seen in that vision, represent the real deceased wicked who are to be raised after the expiration of the millennium: and their resurrection, and their being judged and cast into the lake of fire, foreshow the corresponding real resurrection, judgment, and punishment of that class of persons at that epoch.

Sometimes there is a transition from prophecy

through the medium of symbols, to prophecy through the medium of language. Thus in the fourth chapter of Daniel, after the symbol tree has been spoken of in verses 10–15, there is a transition in the latter part of verse fifteen to Nebuchadnezzar himself, who was the person symbolized by that tree: "Let his portion be with the beasts in the grass of the earth; let his heart be changed from man's, and let a beast's heart be given unto *him;* and let seven times pass over *him.*" Dan. iv. 15, 16. This is a verbal prediction of the seven years' insanity of that king. So also in the second chapter of Daniel, at the thirty-fourth and thirty-fifth verses, a prophecy is given through the medium of symbols. The verbs are all in the past tense; the words are all used in their primary import; and the only figure is a *simile*, in which the broken image is compared to the real and literal chaff of the summer threshing-floors: "Thou sawest till that a stone was cut out without hands, which smote the image upon his feet, that were of iron and clay, and brake them to pieces. Then was the iron, the clay, the brass, the silver, and the gold, broken to pieces together, and became like the chaff of the summer threshing-floors; and the wind carried them away, that no place was found for them; and the stone that smote the image became a great mountain, and filled the whole earth." In verse forty-fourth, however, where we have an inspired explanation of the foregoing prophecy, the same events are predicted through the medium of language: "And in the days of these kings," that is, those who are symbolized by the ten toes, "shall the God of heaven set up a kingdom, which shall never be destroyed: and the kingdom shall not be left to other people, but it shall break in pieces and consume all these kingdoms, and it shall stand for ever."

Sometimes there are verbal statements respecting the future, in connexion with prophetic symbols; as for example, in Rev. xxi. 24, "And the nations of them which are saved *shall walk* in the light of it," the New Jerusalem. Here the verb "*shall walk*," is in the *future* tense, and therefore *cannot be descriptive of a past symbolization*, although *the New Jerusalem* is a *symbol*, and one which had been exhibited to the beloved disciple in the scenic representation mentioned in verses 10–23. As the Lamb is the light of the New Jerusalem, verse twenty-third, the meaning of this prediction is, that these nations shall be guided by the light which Christ gives to those who are denoted by that symbol city—a city which, according to verses 9, 10, represents the same class of persons as "the Bride, the Lamb's wife.*

Let us next observe THE MARKS BY WHICH SYMBOLIC PROPHECIES ARE DISTINGUISHABLE FROM THOSE OF WHICH LANGUAGE IS THE MEDIUM.

The symbolic prophecies are easily distinguished by the fact that *the representative agents or objects were apparently cognizable*, either naturally, or in dreams, or in ecstatic visions, *by some one or more of the bodily senses;* that is, the persons to whom the revelation was symbolically made, *seemed to themselves to see, hear, touch, or taste such agents or objects;* and the language descriptive of such a symbolization, instead of pointing to the future, speaks of the past, namely, of the scenic representation which had been perceptible in the dream, or vision, or otherwise. Nebuchadnezzar, for instance, *saw*, in his dream, a great image which was made of diverse materials, and which was dashed in pieces by a stone that struck it on the feet. Dan. ii. 31–36. St. John, in the sublime visions at Patmos, *saw* a seven-headed and ten-horned beast rising from the sea, Rev. xiii. 1; and *heard*

* See the passage explained more particularly in the eleventh chapter of this essay, under the seventh result.

seven thunders, and *touched* and *tasted* a little book, which was sweet in his mouth, but bitter in his stomach, Rev. x. 3, 4, 8–10. These are evidently symbolic prophecies. In the seventh chapter of the book of Daniel, and at the seventh verse, the prophet says: " After this I *saw* in the night visions, and behold a fourth beast, dreadful, and terrible, and strong exceedingly; and it had great iron teeth; it devoured, and brake in pieces, and stamped the residue with the feet of it; and it was diverse from all the beasts that were before it; and it had ten horns." There is no difficulty in distinguishing this also as a symbolic prophecy. The language simply describes what Daniel saw, and the prediction is made through the medium of the symbols. The "fourth beast," according to the inspired interpretation, verse twenty-third, represented a fourth ruling dynasty, which was to be celebrated for its irresistible prowess and universal dominion.*

On the other hand, when Zechariah says: "The Lord shall be king over all the earth," Zech. xiv. 9; or when Christ says: "They (the Jews) shall fall by the edge of the sword, and shall be led

* In the parallel dream, Dan. ii., the great strength of the fourth dynasty was shown by the iron in the image, Dan. ii. 33, 40.

away captive into all nations; and Jerusalem shall be trodden down of the Gentiles, until the times of the Gentiles be fulfilled," Luke xxi. 24, the prediction is wholly in the language; *for that language, instead of being descriptive of any symbolization, points exclusively to unsymbolic events, which were then future.* In all such prophecies the verbs are commonly in the future tense, though occasionally, for the sake of increased vividness, the present or the past is used for the future. But this is where the general strain of the prophecy shows that a future event is spoken of, and thus furnishes us with the means of avoiding a false interpretation.

Examples might be multiplied to a very great extent, illustrative of the difference between symbolic and verbal prophecy, that is, between prophecy given through the medium of representative agents and objects, and prophecy given through the medium of language; but those which have been already adduced will be sufficient to enable the reader to discriminate between the one class and the other.

CHAPTER II.

CLASSIFICATION OF THE SYMBOLS—PRINCIPLE ON WHICH SYMBOLS ARE EMPLOYED.

THE symbols may be divided into five classes :*

I. LIVING CONSCIOUS AGENTS.

II. DEAD BODIES.

III. NATURAL UNCONSCIOUS AGENTS OR OBJECTS.

IV. ARTIFICIAL OBJECTS.

V. ACTS, EFFECTS, CHARACTERISTICS, CONDITIONS, AND RELATIONS OF AGENTS AND OBJECTS, together with the chronological periods during which certain representative events take place, or a specified agency is exerted, or effects endured by the symbolical subjects of such agency.

We shall mention some examples under each of these classes, and refer to passages of Scripture where they may be found.

I. LIVING CONSCIOUS AGENTS.

1. Divine.

2. Created beings.

* Theological and Literary Journal, edited by David N. Lord, New York. Number for April, 1851, p. 668.

1. Divine: as

God (the Father), Rev. iv. 2, 3; v. 1; xi. 16, 17; xix. 4, called the Ancient of Days, Dan. vii. 9, 13. The Son of God called, in Rev. vi. 1, 16, the Lamb, and in Rev. xix. 13, the Word of God, and in Dan. vii. 13, Rev. i. 13, one like a son of man. (See the Chaldee and Greek.)

2. Created beings.

(1.) *Intelligent.*

(2.) *Unintelligent.*

(1.) *Intelligent created beings:* as

(a.) Living creatures, ζῶα, Rev. iv. 6, 8, 9.

(b.) Angels, Rev. xii. 7.

(c.) Satan or the Devil, Rev. xii. 9, 12; xx. 2, 10.

(d.) Unclean spirits, or spirits of demons, Rev. xvi. 13, 14; fallen angels, Rev. xii. 9.

(e.) Souls, Rev. vi. 9.

(f.) Human beings in the natural life, as the prophet Ezekiel, Ezek. iv. and v.; the prophet Isaiah, Is. xx. 2–4, and the apostle John, Rev. x. 8–11, xi. 1, 2.

(g.) Risen and glorified saints sitting upon thrones, Rev. xx. 4; clothed in fine linen and riding upon white horses, Rev. xix. 14.

(h.) The unholy raised from death, Rev. xx. 15.

(2.) *Unintelligent created beings:* as

(a.) Beasts, such as the bear, Dan. vii. 5; the ram, Dan. viii. 3, 4, 6, 7; the goat, Dan. viii. 5–8.

(b.) Monster animals, such as the winged leopard with four heads, Dan. vii. 6; the ten-horned beast with iron teeth, and nails or claws of brass, Dan. vii. 7, 19; the dragon with sever heads and ten horns, Rev. xii. 3.

(c.) Monster insects, the locusts of the fifth trumpet, which had shapes like horses, faces like the faces of men, hair like the hair of women, teeth like the teeth of lions, and tails like those of scorpions, with stings in their tails, Rev. ix. 7, 8, 10.

II. Dead bodies: as

The slain witnesses, Rev. xi. 8–11.

III. Natural unconscious agents or objects, as

The earth, Rev. xii. 16; the sun, moon, and stars, Rev. viii. 12; waters, Rev. xvii. 15; a burning mountain, Rev. viii. 8; the stone that smote the image, Dan. iii. 34, 35; a tree, Dan. iv. 10–12.

IV. Artificial objects, as

An image, Dan. ii. 31–33; candlesticks, Zech. iv. 2, 3, 11; Rev. i. 12, 13, 20; xi. 4; a sword, Rev. i. 16; vi. 4; xix. 15, 21; cities, such as the great city Babylon, Rev. xvi. 19; and the Holy City, New Jerusalem, Rev. xxi. 2, 10; a crown, *στέφανος* (the badge of victory), Rev. iv. 10; vi. 2; ix. 7; xii. 1; xiv. 14; diadems, *διαδήματα* (the token of dominion), Rev. xii. 3; xiii. 1; xix. 12; books, Dan. vii. 10; Rev. v. 1–5, 7–9; x. 2, 8, 9, 10; xx. 12, 15; white robes, Rev. vi. 11; vii. 9, 13, 14; fine linen, clean and white, Rev. xix. 8, 14.

V. Acts, effects, characteristics, conditions, and relations of agents and objects, as

Speaking, Dan. vii. 8; fighting, Dan. viii. 7;

Rev. xii. 7; being broken to pieces, Dan. ii. 35; ferocity and strength, Dan. vii. 7: heat, Rev. xvi. 9; magnificence and height, Dan. iv. 11, 12; direction, Dan. viii. 4, 5.

To which may be added *chronological periods* during which certain representative events take place, or a specified agency is exerted by the representative agents, or effects endured by the symbolical subjects of such agency; as the three hundred and ninety days during which Ezekiel was to lie on his side for the iniquity of the house of Israel, the forty days during which he was to do the same thing for that of the house of Judah, "each day for a year," Ezek. iv. 5, 6; the forty-two months during which the wild beast from the sea was to exert his characteristic agency, Rev. xiii. 5; the twelve hundred and sixty days during which the witnesses were to prophesy in sackcloth, Rev. xi. 3, previous to their slaughter by the beast from the abyss; and the one thousand years during which Satan was to remain bound and shut up in the abyss, Rev. xx. 2, 3.

The above is, substantially, the classification advocated by Mr. Lord in the Theological and Literary Journal, and it is demonstrably correct, for all the kinds of symbols included in this distribution are found in the sacred Scriptures, and there can be no other than such as these, namely "divine and created; intelligent and unintelligent; living and inanimate; natural and artificial; real and visionary; proper and monstrous;" together with their acts, effects, characteristics, conditions, relations, and chronological periods.

We come next to unfold THE PRINCIPLE ON WHICH SYMBOLS ARE EMPLOYED, and to expound their laws.

If we recur to the symbols which are explained in holy writ, we shall find that in every instance where the symbol and that which it represents are of a different class, species, or order, they are employed on the principle of analogy or resemblance. For example, there is an obvious analogy between a lofty and wide-spreading tree which affords shelter to the fowls of the air, and shade to the beasts of the field, and an illustrious and powerful monarch who gives protection to his subjects and extends his sway over the earth, Dan. iv. 10–27; between a ferocious wild beast which tramples on other animals, and an aggressive dynasty of rulers who exert a corresponding agency towards their adversaries. Dan. vii. 7, 17, 23. In such examples the resemblance is only partial, as a tree is not literally a monarch; nor a beast a man. On the other hand there is, in many instances, a much closer likeness between the symbol and the thing symbolized, as where men in the natural life represent such men, and persons raised from death denote such persons, and in general where the symbolic agents and objects which appeared in the visions represent agents and objects of the same kind or order. This we shall have occasion to show in treating of the LAWS OF SYMBOLIZATION.

CHAPTER III.

SEVEN LAWS OF SYMBOLIZATION—DISCUSSION OF THE FIRST LAW.

I. "THE FIRST LAW: The symbol and that which it represents resemble each other in the station they fill, the relation they sustain, and the agencies they exert in their respective spheres."

II. "THE SECOND LAW: The representative and that which it represents, while the counterpart of each other, are of different species, kinds, or rank, in all cases where the symbol is of such a nature, or is used in such a relation, that it can properly symbolize something different from itself."

III. "THE THIRD LAW: Symbols that are of such a nature, station, or relation, that there is nothing of an analogous kind that they can represent, symbolize agents, objects, acts, or events of their own kind."

IV. "THE FOURTH LAW: When the symbol and that which it symbolizes differ from each other, the correspondence between the representative and that which it represents still extends to their chief parts; and the general elements or parts of the symbol denote corresponding parts in that which is symbolized."

V. "THE FIFTH LAW: The names of symbols are their literal and proper names."

VI. "THE SIXTH LAW: A single agent, in many instances, symbolizes a body and succession of agents."

To these six laws of symbolization enumerated by the editor of the Theological and Literary Journal in the number for April, 1851, may be added for the sake of perspicuity, a seventh, though it is perhaps comprehended in the first.

VII. THE SEVENTH LAW: The periods of time during which a representative agent performs certain representative acts, symbolize the periods during which the agents denoted by the symbols perform the corresponding acts: and, in all cases where such an interpretation is not contrary to analogy, days symbolize years.

The main question at issue, and which it is proposed to settle by this discussion, is, whether these laws are implied in the inspired interpretations of symbols: and to determine that point we must appeal to the Scriptures themselves, and enter upon a fair and candid examination of their contents on the topic before us. It will thus be seen that the above-mentioned laws are all susceptible of a complete demonstration.

I. "The First Law: *The symbol and that which it represents resemble each other in the station they fill, the relation they sustain, and the agencies they exert in their respective spheres.*"

"This is true universally, whether the symbol is employed on the principle of a partial resemblance, or of an exact likeness. Thus an agent symbolizes an agent; an object of agency represents an object of agency; an act denotes an act; an effect foreshows an effect; an office, condition, or characteristic" of the symbol, "an office, condition, or characteristic" of the thing symbolized. "A living agent symbolizes a living agent; a conquering agent denotes a conquering one; a destroying . . one represents a destroyer."

Thus the prophet Ezekiel, in performing certain symbolic acts enjoined upon him, was a symbol of Israel; and in certain others also enjoined upon him, a symbol of Judah. The direction which the Lord gives him is this: "Lie thou also upon thy left side, and lay the iniquity of the house of Israel upon it: according to the number of the days that thou shalt lie upon it, thou shalt bear their iniquity. For I have laid upon thee the years of their iniquity, according to the number of the days, three hundred and ninety days: so shalt thou bear the iniquity of the house of Israel. And when thou hast accomplished them, lie again on thy right side, and thou shalt bear the iniquity of the house of Judah forty days: I have appointed thee each day for a year." Ezek. iv. 4–6. Here Ezekiel, who was himself a living agent, represented the people of Israel and Judah, who were also living agents. In Daniel vii. 3–7, the four great beasts which were living agents, represented four ruling dynasties, which were also living agents. The following is the inspired interpretation: "These great beasts which are four, are four kings," verse 17, that is, they symbolize or represent four kings, or ruling dynasties. So also in the eighth chapter, the ram with two horns, and the he-goat with the great horn between his eyes, themselves living agents, are explained as symbolizing living agents; namely, on the one hand, the Medo-Persian dynasty, and on the other, the Grecian. "The ram which thou sawest having two horns, are the kings of Media and Persia.

And the rough goat is the king of Grecia." Dan. viii. 20, 21. In Zechariah vi. 12, the high priest Joshua, the son of Josedech, a living agent, is a symbol of *the man* Christ Jesus, that is, of the Saviour *in his human nature*, though not a symbol of him in his godhead, which, as is evident from Rev. v., no created agent would be adequate to represent. "Take silver and gold and make crowns, and set them upon the head of Joshua, the son of Josedech, the high priest, and speak unto him, saying: Thus speaketh the Lord of Hosts, saying, Behold THE MAN whose name is THE BRANCH." Zech. vi. 11, 12. The term '*branch*' is here used as a proper name of the man Christ Jesus, with reference to his connexion with the stock of David, as is evident from Jer. xxiii. 5: "Behold the days come, saith the Lord, that I will raise unto David a righteous BRANCH, and a King shall reign and prosper, and shall execute justice in the earth." The seven-headed and ten-horned dragon and wild beast, themselves living agents, symbolized living agents; the seven heads, according to the inspired interpretation, representing "seven kings," or lines of chiefs, of whom, in St. John's time, five had already fallen; and the ten horns, "ten kings," or governors, which were afterwards to arise. "There are seven kings; five are fallen, and one is, and the other is not yet come, and when he cometh, he must continue a short space. . . . And the ten horns which thou sawest are ten kings which have received no kingdom as yet." Rev. xvii. 10, 12.

The inspired interpretation of what was symbolized by the fourth beast, Dan. vii., is another proof of the truth of this law. According to that interpretation, those who were symbolized by that beast were, in their sphere, to exert an agency resembling that which the beast did in his. "After this I saw in the night visions, and behold a fourth beast, dreadful and terrible, and strong exceedingly; and it had great iron teeth; it devoured and brake in pieces, and stamped the residue with the feet of it: and it was diverse from all the beasts that were before it; and it had ten horns." Dan. vii. 7. Such was the symbolization—such the agency of this beast as seen in the vision. Now observe with what exactness the inspired interpretation sustains the law that we are considering. As the fourth beast was a living agent, so were the rulers which that beast symbolized; for it is said of all the four beasts, "These great beasts which are four, are four kings," Dan. vii. 17; and again, "The fourth beast shall be the fourth kingdom upon earth, which shall be diverse from all kingdoms, and shall devour the whole earth, and shall tread down and break it in pieces." Dan. vii. 23. As the fourth beast was diverse from the others, so the fourth ruling dynasty which that beast symbolized, was to be diverse from the others; and as the fourth beast trampled down and brake in pieces the others, and was an all-conquering beast, so the dynasty or line of rulers which it symbolized, was to trample down and break in pieces the others, and to be an all-conquering dynasty. How perfectly, therefore, is the law verified by the inspired interpretation. In all these examples living agents represent living agents, and so in all the interpreted symbols of the Hebrew prophets.

The dream of Pharaoh, concerning the seven fat and the seven lean kine, is an exception to the general principle, that living agents represent living agents; but inasmuch as it is explained in the Scriptures, it presents no practical embarrassment; and being in accordance with the arbitrary hieroglyphics among the Egyptians, and thus far, according to the ordering of God's providence, taking its complexion, perhaps, from the monarch's waking thoughts, it is not to be considered as setting aside the laws which govern the interpretation of the symbolical image and stone, Dan. ii., and the symbolical tree, Dan. iv., or the symbols which were perceptible naturally, and used by the Hebrew prophets under the Lord's direction, or those which were exhibited to them in dream or vision.

Again: while living agents in all such cases never symbolize inanimate objects, it is equally true that in many instances, inanimate objects that act or exert agencies, do represent—on the principle of general resemblance or analogy—living agents. The one exert in their sphere an agency analogous to that which the others exert in theirs. Thus, in Rev. i. 20, the seven candlesticks, or lamp-stands, symbolize seven churches, assemblies, or congregations of living men, ἐκκλησίαι; and the seven stars, seven messengers of the churches. A candlestick or lamp-stand supporting a lamp which gives light in the circle around it, is an appropriate symbol of a church or congregation of worshippers, which supports a religious teacher who sheds the light of divine truth in the circle of his ministrations. The stars, on the same principle of analogy, are suitable emblems of sacred messengers, ministers of the gospel commissioned by God, and sent by the churches to preach the word and administer religious instruction, warning, or consolation. The term ἄγγελος being here used in the same connexion with ἐκκλησία, the one as an explanation of what is denoted by the stars, and the other of what is meant by the candlesticks, is doubtless to be taken in its primary import of *messenger*, and not in the secondary import of *angel*, a being belonging to a rank of intelligences superior to man, and deriving this name from his office. The stone from the mountain, Dan. ii. 34, 45, which smote the image on the feet, and brake it in pieces, is explained in the context, as denoting the kings whom God is to establish in his kingdom, and who, in demolishing the dynasties represented by the ten toes, are to exert in their sphere an agency analogous to that which in its corresponding sphere was exerted by the stone. "In the days of these kings shall the God of heaven set up a kingdom which shall never be destroyed, and the kingdom shall not be left to other people, but it shall break in pieces, and consume all these kingdoms, and it shall stand for ever." Dan. ii. 44. The stone strikes the image on the feet, and of course on the ten toes, and crushes it: the meaning of which is, that those whom the stone symbolizes, are at the time appointed, to wit, at an epoch subsequent to the division of the fourth great monarchy into ten kingdoms, to overturn with resistless might, and utterly demolish the opposing dynasties, and establish their own everlasting kingdom upon the wreck and ruin of these antagonistic sovereignties; just as the stone, with great violence and overwhelming force, utterly broke in pieces the symbolic image, which "became like the chaff of the summer threshing-floors," and was carried away by the wind, "that no place was found for" it. Dan. ii. 35. That what was thus true of the symbol is also true of the dynasty which it represented, is clearly indicated in the inspired interpretation, by the words, "*break in pieces*," and "*consume*," Dan. ii. 44; which denote, in this connexion, not reformation, but destruction. Similar language had just before been used, Dan. ii. 40, to signify the crushing force with which the dynasty represented in that chapter by the iron and clay, and in the seventh by the fourth beast, was to overwhelm its opponents; and here also it must have the same meaning.

From these inspired interpretations it is evident that an object of agency denotes such an object, and an effect in the symbol foreshows a like effect in the thing symbolized. Thus the image, which was dashed to pieces by the stone, represented the dynasties which are to be destroyed by those whom the stone symbolizes. The agency of the stone foreshowed the analogous agency of the corresponding dynasty; and the effect produced by the one, the analogous effect which is to be accomplished by the other. So the act of the fourth beast in trampling down and devouring other animals signified that of the symbolized rulers in crushing and destroying their antagonists: and the slaying of that beast and the burning of its body denoted the utter destruction of those whom the beast represented.

We have thus proved the first law by the symbolic agency of the prophet Ezekiel, Ezek. iv., and that of Joshua the son of Josedech the high priest, Zech. vi., by the four great beasts, Dan. vii., the ram with the two horns, Dan. viii., the seven-headed and ten-horned dragon and wild beast, Rev. xii. xvii., the seven candlesticks and seven stars, Rev. i., and the stone and the image, Dan. ii. We have therefore, in these inspired interpretations, contained in the word of God, the most complete demonstration of the truth of the law—that *the symbol and that which it represents resemble each other in the station they fill, the relation they sustain, and the agencies they exert in their respective spheres.*

CHAPTER IV.

Discussion of the second law.

II. "The Second Law: *The representative and that which it represents, while the counterpart of each other, are of different spheres, kinds, or rank, in all cases where the symbol is of such a nature, or is used in such a relation, that it can properly symbolize something different from itself:*"—or, in other words, the symbol, where the nature of the case admits, is of a different class or order from that which is symbolized, as, for example, a *beast* is of a different order from a *king;* a *military* or *political* chieftain, in his appropriate sphere, as such, is of a different order, class, or rank, from an *ecclesiastical* ruler: but in these cases the analogy between the symbol and that which it represents is always preserved.

Thus the ram and the he-goat, Dan. viii., according to the inspired interpretation, did not symbolize a herd or succession of rams and he-goats; but these animals, leaders of their respective flocks and antagonists of each other, symbolize agents of a different order, namely, not brutes but men, chieftains who contended the one against the other, in a manner analogous to that exhibited in the symbols. So in the great image, Dan. ii., the head of gold, according to the inspired interpretation, did not symbolize a collection of metallic heads, but objects of a different kind, to wit, a dynasty of men who were to be succeeded by other dynasties of men represented by the other parts of the image. The four beasts, Dan. vii., according to the inspired interpretation, did not denote a herd or succession of beasts, but agents of a different order, namely, aggressive dynasties of civil rulers, who in their sphere were the counterpart of what the wild beasts were in theirs. The waters, Rev. xvii. 15, according to the inspired interpretation, did not symbolize a collection of waters, but a vast multitude of people belonging to different nations and speaking different languages. "The waters which thou sawest, where the harlot sitteth, are peoples, and multitudes, and nations, and tongues." The seven candlesticks and seven stars, Rev. i. 12, 16, 20, according to the inspired interpretation, did not represent a collection of candlesticks and stars, but churches or congregations of men, and religious teachers who were the messengers of the churches. "The seven stars are the messengers of the seven churches: and the seven candlesticks which thou sawest are the seven churches," Rev. i. 20. Michael and his angels warring in the sky with Satan* and *his* angels, Rev. xii. 7–9, do not symbolize beings of the angelic order, but those of a different order, to wit, living *men* of the epoch denoted, that is, believers in Christ on the one hand and hostile pagans on the other. This is evident from verse tenth, where persons of the human species, representing those who had been symbolized by victorious Michael and his angels, are introduced in vision, according to the next law which we shall notice, and exhibited as saying—"Now is come salvation, and strength, and the kingdom of our God, and the power of his Christ: for the

* Satan, the fallen angel, who is called the dragon, that old serpent the Devil; and who is used as a symbol in verses 7–9, must not be confounded with the great red dragon having seven heads and ten horns, with diadems on the heads, a monster having only a visionary existence, who is used as a symbol in verse 3, and who represents the civil rulers of the Roman empire antecedently to its division into ten kingdoms, and, after that division, the civil rulers of the Eastern or Græco-Roman empire.

accuser of our brethren is cast down, which accused them before our God day and night:" and then follows the statement—"and they overcame him by THE BLOOD OF THE LAMB, and by the word of their testimony; and they loved not their lives unto the death," verse 11. This clearly shows that those who had been symbolized in verses 7–9, were not of the same order as Michael and Satan, but of a different order; *not angels, but men:* for the latter and not the former are subject to death, and become victorious through the blood of Christ. Heb. ii. 15, 16. These examples from Scripture with the inspired interpretations conclusively show that, *under the condition specified in the law*, the symbol is always of a different kind or order from that which is symbolized: and that there is an analogy between the one and the other has already been proved in the discussion of the first law.

There are cases in which any other construction is utterly impossible, consistently with the truth of the prophecy. Take one instance as a sample of the rest. In Rev. xii. 3, 4, the symbolic representation is—"And there appeared another wonder in heaven; and behold a great red dragon, having seven heads and ten horns, and seven diadems, διαδήματα, upon his heads.

And his tail drew the third part of the stars of heaven, and did cast them to the earth." No one supposes that these symbols are to be verified in any real literal dragon of this description, of such gigantic size and force as literally to sweep down with his tail a third of the stars from the sky to the earth. Such a supposition would be absurd and incredible. They denote therefore analogous agents of a different order. We might examine in like manner other symbols of the Apocalypse, and show the same thing in regard to them which is manifest at once in regard to the example just cited.

Hence this law refutes the erroneous interpretations which have extensively prevailed with respect to the first four seals. Rev. vi. 1–8. The symbolic horsemen of those seals are evidently taken from military and political life, and they have frequently been regarded as representing classes of persons of the same order as the symbols. But according to the law that we have just demonstrated, the agents thus represented are not of the same, but of a different order. We are therefore to look for them not in the military and political, but in the religious world. Hence the warrior of the first seal who carries a bow and wears a crown, στέφανος, the badge of victory, and rides upon a white horse, symbolizes faithful and successful *ministers of the gospel.* The age immediately following that of the apostles was distinguished for ministers who gloried in winning trophies for Christ, and converting their fellow-men to the knowledge of the truth: and these and their successors of like character were represented by the symbolic horseman of the first seal, the rider on the white horse, who "went forth conquering and to conquer." Rev. vi. 2. But in the subsequent ages other clergy arose of very different character and doings—"the ambitious and contentious, who usurped an unauthorized dominion over the church, and distracted and wasted it by strifes and misrule,"—also "the unfaithful and treacherous, who perverted their office to the suppression and adulteration of the truth, and reduced their flocks to famine and misery:"—and lastly, those who "introduced new objects of homage, a new worship and new conditions of pardon, rendered their teachings a moral pestilence that taints and kills all who fall under its power, and made . . . the civil rulers . . . their instruments in the work of destruction."* And these

* Lord's Exposition of the Apocalypse, pp. 152, 153.

ministers and their successors of similar disposition and conduct are represented by the symbolic horsemen of the second, third, and fourth seals, the riders on the red, black, and pale horses. Rev. vi. 4, 5, 8.

It may be thought at the first view, that the four symbol horses are exceptions to the general law, that living agents denote living agents. If that be so, the exception in each case relates to the subordinate part of a complex symbol, and must be treated accordingly, as necessary to exhibit the symbol riders in the attitude of military or civil officers who, as we have just explained, are employed in the vision to represent leaders of a different order, to wit, ministers of religion. But it cannot be shown that the four horses *are* exceptions to the general law.* The horses were of course auxiliaries to their respective riders, and therefore, for aught that appears to the contrary, may symbolize the men who sustained an

* Mr. Cuninghame, in expounding the first seal, says: "The rider on the horse may be understood to signify the rulers or ministers, and the horse the body of the church."—Cuninghame on the Apocalypse, pp. 5, 6. London, 1832, Third Edition.

The symbolic horsemen of the second, third, and fourth seals also, he considers as representing ecclesiastical rulers.—Ib., pp. 7–19.

analogous relation to the ministers represented by those riders:—just as the ten-horned beast in the seventeenth chapter symbolizes the auxiliaries of those who are represented by the harlot sorceress that rode on that beast:—living agents denoting living agents, and where the nature of the case admits, those of a different order or kind.

From what has been already said, it is abundantly evident—and the truth of the remark will be more fully exemplified as we proceed—that there are definite principles of interpretation clearly implied in the inspired volume, which should govern the exposition of prophetic symbols; and therefore this whole subject, instead of being, as many suppose, vague, uncertain, and indeterminate, is controlled by well established laws; and God's word in all its parts, the symbolic as well as the unsymbolic, contains what is properly called a revelation, or disclosure of the high counsels of heaven in regard to the condition and prospects of men.

The second law, therefore, of prophetic symbols, as well as the first, we have fully verified by the inspired interpretations. We have proved it by a reference to the ram and the he-goat, Dan. viii.; the great image, Dan. ii.; the four beasts, Dan. vii.; the waters, Rev. xvii.; the seven candlesticks and the seven stars, Rev. i.; Michael and his angels, and Satan and the fallen angels, and the great red dragon, Rev. xii.; and illustrated its utility by an application of it to the first four seals, Rev. vi. The law, therefore, has been not merely exhibited, but fully demonstrated by the authority of God's sacred word, agreeably to the line of argument and discussion which we proposed to adopt in this essay; and therefore it may be regarded as a revealed principle or law, that *the representative and that which it represents, while the counterpart of each other, are of different spheres, kinds, or rank, in all cases, where the symbol is of such a nature, or is used in such a relation, that it can properly symbolize something different from itself.*

CHAPTER V.

Discussion of the third law.

III. "The Third Law: *Symbols that are of such a nature, station, or relation, that there is nothing of an analogous kind that they can represent, symbolize agents, objects, acts, or events of their own kind.*"

Thus in Rev. v., the Lamb, the incarnate Son of God, appears in the vision as his own representative, because in respect to his deity in union with humanity, and the peculiar relations which he sustains, and acts which he performs as a divine person, he could not properly be represented by any created agent. The terms, "*Lamb*," "*Lion of the tribe of Judah*," "*Root of David*," are here used as *Proper Names* of the Son of God. That these are appropriate denominatives of the Messiah, will not be questioned, and that Jesus Christ himself is the Lamb here spoken of, is evident from the context, where it is said: "And he came and took the book out of the right hand of him that sat upon the throne. And when he had taken the book, the four living creatures, ζῶα, and four-and-twenty elders fell down before THE LAMB, having every one of them harps, and golden vials full of odors, which are the prayers of saints. And they sang a new song, saying, THOU art worthy to take the book, and to open the seals thereof; for THOU WAST SLAIN, AND HAST REDEEMED US to God by thy blood, out of every kindred, and tongue, and people, and nation; and hast made us unto our God kings and priests; and we shall reign on the earth." Rev. v. 7–10. None but Jesus Christ has performed the work of redemption, and to none but him would such a song be applicable. None but a divine person could rightly be associated with God the Father in such an ascription of praise as that in verse 13th: "Blessing, and honor, and glory, and power, be unto him that sitteth upon the throne, and unto *the Lamb* for ever and ever." To have paid such adoration* to a mere creature,

* See the full exhibition of the worship rendered to the Lamb, Rev. v. 8–13, and compare Rev. xiv. 1, where God is alluded to as the "Father" of the Lamb: "And I looked, and lo, the *Lamb** stood on the mount Sion, and with him an hundred forty and four thousand, having *his* FATHER'S *name* written in their foreheads." Surely, *the Son of the Father* must be Christ, *the Lamb* of God, and not a mere brute animal.

* The best editions have here, Rev. xiv. 1, τὸ ἀρνίον, *the* Lamb.

whether a lamb or any other animal, would have been as much an act of idolatry, as that of the children of Israel when they proclaimed a festival unto Jehovah, and worshipped a golden calf as the representative of the great God who had brought them up out of the land of Egypt. Exod. xxxii. 4, 5, 6, 8. It is no mere created agent, therefore, but the almighty and divine Redeemer, the risen and glorified Saviour, who is here presented to us as *the Lamb* whom saints and angels worship. The symbolic appendages of seven horns and seven eyes, Rev. v. 6, which John saw in the vision, were doubtless assumed for the occasion, as emblematical of Christ's omnipotent and omnipresent Spirit in its sevenfold or complete and entire perfection—the Holy Spirit of God.

This epithet, therefore, the "*Lamb*," is in that vision *a denominative of the Lord Jesus Christ*, as it is in Rev. vi. 16, where "the kings of the earth" and others "said to the mountains and rocks, Fall on us and hide us from the face of him that sitteth on the throne, and from the wrath of *the Lamb*;" and in Rev. vii. 14, 17, where it is said of the white-robed palm-bearers, that they have "washed their robes and made them white in the blood of *the Lamb*"—and that "*the Lamb* which is *in the midst of the throne*" (compare Rev. v. 6, where the Lamb is spoken of as occupying, in that vision, the same position, namely, "*in the midst of the throne*")—"*the Lamb* which is *in the midst of the throne* shall feed them, and shall lead them unto living fountains of waters."*

The omission of the article in the Greek of Rev. v. 6, does not seem, when we examine the context, a sufficient reason for the opinion that the being whom John saw in the vision was a mere brute animal. The Lamb spoken of stood by the throne of God, Rev. v. 6; he came and took the book from the right hand of him who sat upon the throne, verse 7th; he received the worship of the heavenly hosts, verse 8th; and the reason assigned in the "new song" why he was worthy to take the book and open the seals

* Compare John i. 29, 35, 36: "The next day John seeth *Jesus* coming unto him, and saith, Behold *the Lamb* of God which taketh away the sin of the world." "Again, the next day after, John stood, and two of his disciples; and looking upon *Jesus* as he walked, he saith, Behold *the Lamb* of God."

There can be no question, therefore, that the term *Lamb* might properly be used in the Apocalypse, as a denominative of the Lord Jesus Christ; and if the Lamb *in the midst of the throne*, as spoken of in Rev. vii. 17, is *Christ*, so also is the Lamb *in the midst of the throne*, as spoken of in Rev. v. 6.

thereof, was because he had been slain, and had redeemed them to God by his blood, verse 9th; which shows that Christ was the person addressed. The visible indications that Christ the Lamb had been slain, Rev. v. 6, consisted, perhaps, of the marks on his person, such as the print of the nails in his hands and his feet, and the impression of the spear in his wounded side, marks which, it will be recollected, were visible in the resurrection body in which he appeared to the disciples, John xx. 27; and in which he ascended to heaven, Luke xxiv. 39, 40, 51; Acts i. 9.

The term *Lamb*, therefore, in these passages, is to be taken as a *Proper Name* of our Lord Jesus Christ, *the Lamb that was slain*, Rev. xiii. 8.

In like manner in Rev. xix. 11–21, Christ appears as his own representative. This is evident from the description there given. He is styled "THE WORD OF GOD," verse 13th, a name which, in the first chapter of St. John's gospel, is applied to that divine person, the Eternal Son of God, who took human nature into union with himself. "He hath on his vesture and on his thigh a name written, KING *of kings and* LORD *of lords*," verse 16th; compare Rev. xvii. 14. He has "a sharp sword" proceeding from his mouth, one of the symbolic badges of the risen Saviour, in Rev. i. 16, indicative of the fact that his avenging sentence is to result in the destruction of his enemies; "and HE TREADETH THE WINE PRESS of the fierceness and wrath of Almighty God," verse 15th. Hence his characteristic as an Avenger in that day, is symbolized in verse 13th, by the raiment in which he is clothed—"A VESTURE DIPPED IN BLOOD." There can be no question, therefore, that the Leader of the heavenly armies, Rev. xix. 11–21, is the risen and glorified Saviour. He cannot be a mere "personification of Christianity." Such an exposition is wholly at variance with the symbolization, which evidently represents *a living agent.* As well might it be said that the ram and the he-goat, Dan. viii., are mere personifications of war. If the one symbolized "*the kings of Media and Persia,*" Dan. viii. 20, and the other, "*the king of Grecia,*" verse 21, as we are expressly told in the inspired interpretation of that vision, so this celestial Leader is shown, with equal clearness, by his name and characteristics, to be the "KING *of kings and Lord of lords,*" Rev. xix. 16; the personal "WORD OF GOD," verse 13, the Lord Jesus Christ.

For a similar reason, namely, because no

created agent could properly represent him, God the Father also symbolizes himself.

Thus in Rev. iv., the person seated on the throne in heaven, verse 2d, and who is distinguished from the Lamb that came to him, Rev. v. 7, is evidently God the Father, for he receives the adoration of saints and angels, Rev. v. 13, and holds in his hand a book, Rev. v. 1, symbolical of the divine purposes, and written within and without to show that those purposes are complete and full, a book which none but the Lamb can take and open, Rev. v. 2–7, he being the Revealer of the counsels of the deity.

In Rev. vii. 9–17, the white-robed palm-bearers symbolize those victorious believers who come out of the great tribulation—*οὗτοί εἰσιν οἱ ἐρχόμενοι ἐκ τῆς θλίψεως τῆς μεγάλης*, literally translated—"THESE ARE THEY WHO COME FROM OUT OF THE TRIBULATION THE GREAT." Rev. vii. 14, compare Dan. xii. 1, Rev. xvi. 18. They are manifestly individuals of the human race who are believers in Christ, because none but such can be said to wash their garments "in the blood of the Lamb," verse 14. As the persons indicated are those WHO COME OUT OF THE GREAT TRIBULATION, they can only be those WHO WERE ONCE IN IT, and are therefore believers who, after having lived at the epoch denoted by the vision, and continued faithful to their trust in the midst of unprecedented trouble, are to rejoice, as here represented, in their ultimate deliverance. They are clothed in white robes to show that they are accepted before God: and they bear the palm in token of victory. They enjoy the beatific presence of their God and Saviour, for they are "before the throne of God, and serve him day and night in his temple: and he that sitteth on the throne shall dwell among them. They shall hunger no more, neither thirst any more; neither shall the sun strike them, πέσῃ ἐπ' αὐτοὺς, nor any heat. For the Lamb which is in the midst of the throne shall feed them, and shall lead them unto living fountains of waters: and God shall wipe away all tears from their eyes." Rev. vii. 15–17. In other words, they are to be exempt from all evil, to be clothed with immortality, to have the most delightful communion with their heavenly Father, to receive the visible manifestations of his personal presence, and to be for ever with Jesus. The glory of their deliverance—ἡ σωτηρία, "THE SALVATION"—they ascribe with adoring gratitude to "God which sitteth upon the throne and unto the Lamb," verse 10. They are symbolized in the vision by those of their own order, for no others can properly represent them as performing the acts and receiving the rewards here specified.

The spirits of the martyrs under the fifth seal symbolize such spirits, for disembodied spirits, in the intermediate state between death and the resurrection, calling upon God for retribution, could not appropriately be represented by any persons except those of their own order or species. "And when he had opened the fifth seal, I saw under the altar the souls of them that were slain for the word of God, and for the testimony which they held: and they cried with a loud voice saying, How long, O Lord, holy and true, dost thou not judge and avenge our blood on them that dwell on the earth? And white robes were given unto every one of them; and it was said unto them, that they should rest yet for a little season, until their fellow servants also and their brethren that should be killed, as they were, should be fulfilled," Rev. vi. 9–11. The souls here spoken of are departed spirits of good men who, at the epoch denoted by the vision, had been slain for their fidelity to the truth: for they are the souls of those who had suffered martyrdom "for the word of God, and for the testimony which they held:" they are clothed in white robes, which denotes that they are accepted before God: and the period at which the persons represented utter the cry is anterior to the resurrection, for the symbol spirits are told to rest for a little season until the number of martyrs should be complete.

The men spoken of in Rev. vi. 15, 16, also symbolize those of their own order, for there was no other way to represent individual human beings in the natural life performing the acts there mentioned. "And the kings of the earth, and the great men, and the rich men, and the chief captains, and the mighty men, and every bondman, and every freeman, hid themselves in the dens and in the rocks of the mountains; and said to the mountains and rocks, Fall on us and hide us from the face of him that sitteth on the throne, and from the wrath of the Lamb: for the great day of his wrath is come; and who shall be able to stand?" Rev. vi. 15–17.

The witnesses in Rev. xi., represented, for a similar reason, persons of their own order. The statement in verse 3 is—"I will give* unto my two witnesses," (that is, I will bestow upon them the gifts requisite for their office and work) "and

* The word *power* in the common English version, Rev. xi. 3, is not in the original Greek.

they shall prophesy a thousand two hundred and threescore days, clothed in sackcloth;" that is, they shall, in a state of depression and humiliation, continue to proclaim the truth as it is in Jesus throughout that entire period. The witnesses are explained in verse 4, to represent *the same as* might be symbolized by *two olive trees and two candlesticks.* A candlestick, as we learn from Rev. i. 20, is the symbol of a *church.* These "candlesticks," therefore, Rev. xi. 4, denote *churches* which bear a faithful testimony to the truth as it is in Jesus throughout the whole period symbolized by the twelve hundred and sixty days. Rev. xi. 2, 3. The "*olive trees,*" as we learn from Zech. iv. 3, 12, 14, denote the "anointed ones that stand by the Lord of the whole earth," that is, priests or ministers of the Lord, and, in this connexion, ministers of the churches here symbolized. In ancient times priests were set apart for their office by being anointed with oil, and hence they are called "anointed ones." It would be incongruous, however, to represent candlesticks and olive trees as prophesying or as being slain and rising from the dead and ascending to heaven: and hence, in order to exhibit them in such relations, the followers of Christ here referred to, both ministers and people, are symbolized by two individual men, called *witnesses* in verse third, and *prophets* in verse tenth, persons of their own species, to whom such acts and conditions are, in all respects, appropriate.

The "anointed ones" here indicated cannot mean the persecuting civil rulers, for these are symbolized by the wild beast who makes war upon them and slays them; and they are evidently persons who testify for Christ; and therefore as the candlesticks would symbolize churches, the anointed ones, corresponding to the olive trees, must mean ministers, and, doubtless, the ministers of those churches.

If the number *two* be interpreted according to the use of the number *seven* in Rev. i. 20, "the *seven* candlesticks which thou sawest are the *seven* churches," to wit, the seven in pro-consular Asia mentioned in a previous verse of the same chapter, Rev. i. 11, Ephesus, Smyrna, Pergamos, Thyatira, Sardis, Philadelphia, and Laodicea—then *two* candlesticks, if used as symbols, would represent *two* churches; and *two* olive trees would indicate *two* lines or successions of ministers, namely, the ministers of those two churches: and consequently, in that case, the *two* witnesses" would represent two sets of witnesses, the *pastors* and *people* of the churches symbolized, as already explained.

If, however, we adopt the opinion that the number *two* is here used simply because two are necessary to make out a *complete* testimony (compare Matt. xviii. 16)—as the number *seven* in Rev. v. 6, taken in connexion with the symbolic horns and eyes, ("*seven* horns and *seven* eyes, which are the *seven* spirits of God,") denotes the *sevenfold* or *complete* omnipotence and omnipresence of the Holy Spirit of the incarnate Deity—if we take this view, the result will not vary much from that given above. The two witnesses will then represent all the churches of faithful believers with their pastors, who, during the period symbolized by the twelve hundred and sixty days, and in the localities to which the prophecy has reference, bear the testimony, and exert, in other respects, the agency here foreshown.

But whether we take the one view or the other, we must rank, among the witnesses here represented, the church of the Waldenses or *Vallenses*, a people whose name is derived from their residence, and signifies *men of the valleys*.*

* Some writers have fallen into the error of representing them as deriving their name from Peter Waldo. The incor-

"The Christian religion which was planted in Italy by Paul has ever since been retained in the primitive purity of its fundamental doctrine . . . in the churches of Piedmont to this day."* That line of faithful witnesses exists to the present time. The little remnant of the martyr race is still flourishing in Sardinia, but—regarded with an evil eye by deadly, unrelenting, and powerful enemies—the way seems preparing for their final slaughter.†

The learned Peter Allix, a French Protestant divine who flourished in the reign of Louis the Fourteenth, and took refuge in England after the revocation of the edict of Nantes, in his

rectness of that opinion has been shown by Allix, Faber, and others. See especially the Ecclesiastical History of the Ancient Churches of Piedmont by Peter Allix, D.D., chapter xviii, pp. 182, 183, and chapter xix. Oxford ed. 8vo. 1821; and Faber's Ancient Vallenses and Albigenses, pp. 271–531. London, 1838.

* History of the Ancient Christians inhabiting the valleys of the Alps, from the works of Jean Paul Perrin and Dr. Bray, with illustrative notes from modern historians and theologians, published by Griffith and Simon, Philadelphia, 1847. Preface to Part iii. p. 275.

† The liberality of Victor Emanuel, in granting them permission to build a church edifice in Turin, is no proof that hostile powers will suffer them to enjoy a perpetuity of civil and religious freedom.

Ecclesiastical History of the Ancient Churches of Piedmont, has traced the Waldenses to the age immediately succeeding that of the apostles; vindicated the purity of their morals; successfully defended them from the charge of heresy and schism; and shown that they maintained their faith until the Reformation:* and if Rome inquires of Protestants, where was your church before the time of Luther, we answer it was in ancient Britain,† in Italy and Gaul, protesting against the corruptions of the great Apostacy, its faith derived from the apostles and continuing to the present time.

But without enlarging upon the historical exposition, which would take us too far from the

* The Rev. George Stanley Faber has given a similar vindication of these faithful Christians in his work referred to in a previous note and entitled—"An Inquiry into the History and Theology of the ancient Vallenses and Albigenses; as exhibiting, agreeably to the promises, the perpetuity of the sincere church of Christ." London, 1838. His Romish antagonist, the acute and learned Bossuet, cuts but a sorry figure in the hands of the Anglican divine.

† Not only on the continent of Europe but in Britain also, as D'Aubigné has shown in the fifth volume of his History of the Reformation, Christ had a church previous to the first introduction of popery into that country by the monk Augustine, A.D. 597,—a church which manfully resisted the usurpations of Rome.

main point under discussion, we sum up our remarks upon the question, as to who are symbolized by the apocalyptic witnesses, by observing that *two circumstances are necessary to identify any churches and their line of pastors with those witnesses: first, they must exist throughout the entire period symbolized by the twelve hundred and sixty days*, Rev. xi. 3; *and next, they must bear a faithful testimony for Christ during the whole of that same period, and in the localities to which the prophecy refers.*

But in regard to the reason for using the number *two* in its application to the *witnesses*, *prophets*, *candlesticks*, and *olive trees*, Rev. xi. 3, 10, 4, there is room, perhaps, for difference of opinion as to whether it be designed to point out *two* collections of churches and their respective lines of pastors, or simply intended to indicate the fact that the churches and pastors symbolized, bear *a complete testimony*, and constitute A COMPLETE CHAIN OF FAITHFUL WITNESSES.

To return to the third law of symbolization, we remark further in its support, that in Rev. xii. 10, the servants of Christ, who in verse seventh had been symbolized by celestial beings, are represented by some of their own species, because it would have been incorrect to speak of Michael and his angels as overcoming by the blood of the Lamb, and as loving not their lives unto the death, verse 11th; for angels and archangels are neither subject to death, nor redeemed by the blood of Christ.

In Rev. xiii. 4, the men who are exhibited in the vision as worshipping the beast, symbolize persons of the human species, for those who perform the corresponding acts of idolatrous subservience to those whom the beast represents, could properly be exhibited in that relation only by those of their own kind. To have introduced angels, either fallen or unfallen, as engaged in worshipping a beast, would have been a needless incongruity, and hence they are not employed as the representatives of men in their idolatry of civil rulers; to have used rivers, or fountains, or a sea of waters, in that symbolic relation of worshippers of a beast, would obviously have been impossible: to have exhibited the beast as worshipped by other beasts, would have been a false symbolization, for the object here is to foreshow that a collection of rulers would be worshipped by the great mass of the population over whom they reign, and not that those rulers would be worshipped by other rulers; and therefore the mass of the people are here represented by those of their own species.

The same may be said of the men spoken of in Rev. ix. 4, who had not the seal of God in their foreheads, and those in verses 20, 21, who repented not of their idolatries and other sins.

The same also of the men who, under the scorching effects of the fourth vial, Rev. xvi. 9, "Blasphemed the name of God . . . and repented not to give him glory." Blaspheming and impenitent men could be properly represented in that character only by such men.

The same may be said of the men who are spoken of in connexion with some of the other vials, Rev. xvi. 2, 11, 21.

In Rev. xvi. 14, "The kings (or rulers) of the whole world,"* represent persons of their own order. Those persons could not appropriately be symbolized by the wild beast, which represented only the rulers of a particular part of the world; and in Rev. xix. 19, where the same war is spoken of as in Rev. xvi. 14, 16, that to which

* The best editions of the Greek Testament omit the τῆς γῆς καὶ of the textus receptus, and instead of "the kings *of the earth and* of the whole world," read simply "*the kings of the whole world.*"

the "three unclean spirits" gathered* those kings, we read of "the beast AND the kings of the earth." The symbolization, therefore, was designed to include other rulers besides those denoted by the beast. Neither the beast, nor the dragon, nor the false prophet, nor all combined, could represent "the kings of *the whole world.*" It was therefore necessary that they should be their own representatives.

In Rev. xx. 1–3, the angel who laid hold upon Satan, represents good angels; and Satan, fallen

* There is an inaccuracy in our common English Version in Rev. xvi. 16, which obscures the sense, and which has arisen from overlooking the principle of Greek Grammar, that *nominatives plural of the neuter gender have commonly a singular verb.* The phrase rendered, "And *he* gathered them," should have been translated, "And THEY gathered them," that is, *the three unclean spirits gathered them,* πνεύματα τρία, in verse 13th, being the antecedent of the pronoun in the nominative plural neuter understood before the verb συνήγαγεν, in verse 16th. They are spoken of in verse 14th as going forth "unto the kings of the whole world TO GATHER them to the battle of that great day of God Almighty." In that very verse, Rev. xvi. 14, there is a similar construction in the original Greek; ἃ (= which), a pronoun in the neuter plural, nominative to the verb ἐκπορεύεται (= go forth), in the third person singular. The 15th verse is parenthetical, and the 16th is connected with the 14th. The three unclean spirits, therefore, symbolize the agents who gather the kings to the war of "Armageddon." Rev. xvi. 14, 16.

angels. "And I saw an angel come down from heaven, having the key of the bottomless pit, and a great chain in his hand. And he laid hold on the dragon, that old serpent, which is the Devil and Satan, and bound him a thousand years, and cast him into the bottomless pit, and shut him up and set a seal upon him, that he should deceive the nations no more, till the thousand years should be fulfilled: and after that he must be loosed a little season."

The person here styled the "dragon, that old serpent which is the Devil and Satan," is not the red dragon of seven heads and ten horns which symbolized the rulers of the Roman Empire previous to its division into ten kingdoms, but the leader and chief of the fallen angels: nor does he here symbolize hostile pagans, as in Rev. xii. 7–9, but beings of his own kind. To prevent the domination of sin during the millennium, it would seem necessary not merely that Satan himself, but also the other fallen angels, should be prevented throughout that period from deceiving the nations. Hence Satan here represents not only himself, but also others of the same order: and this symbolization was requisite, because in these circumstances they could not appropriately be represented by men, or by any other beings except one of their own class.

It is asserted, however, that in Rev. xx. 2, 3, Satan symbolizes an antichristian party among men. But he cannot there symbolize such a party, for they as an organized confederacy were represented, Rev. xix. 19–21, by the wild beast and the false prophet and the kings of the earth and their armies who had been destroyed: and as he is shut up during the millennium "in the bottomless pit," or abyss, which symbolizes the place of his confinement throughout that period, and not released until after its expiration, no such party can, during that cycle of ages, be re-organized on the earth, the nations being exempted, until after the thousand years are ended, from temptation by those symbolized by Satan. Rev. xx. 2, 3, 7, 8.

So on the other hand the antagonist angel, who laid hold upon Satan the representative of the fallen angels who were to be subjected to the agency here indicated, symbolizes persons of *his* order. The work performed by the symbolic angel required an angel's strength: and therefore to have represented men as performing it would have been a false symbolization. Good angels, in exerting the agency here foreshown, could properly be symbolized only by one of their own order: and evil angels, in being subject to such an agency, could be represented only by one of theirs.

In Rev. xx. 12–15, we read: "And I saw the dead, small and great, stand before God; and the books were opened: and another book was opened which is the book of life: and the dead were judged out of those things which were written in the books according to their works. And the sea gave up the dead which were in it; and death and hell delivered up the dead which were in them: and they were judged every man according to their works. And death and hell were cast into the lake of fire. This is the second death. And whosoever was not found written in the book of life was cast into the lake of fire."

We have already shown that this is a symbolical vision describing what St. John saw, and therefore that the prophecy here is through the medium of symbols. Otherwise the passage contains no prophecy whatever, but only narrates a past event. It is generally admitted that a real resurrection is here foreshown: *and what other than a real, corporeal resurrection could that be which is to take place in connexion with the judgment before the "great white throne?"* verse 11. When therefore St. John says that he saw the dead, small and great, stand before God, the risen dead, seen in the vision, manifestly symbolize the risen dead of the epoch denoted. They are called *dead*, because it will then be true that those represented have been dead: and therefore the epithet is used to identify the class of persons referred to, not that they were to continue dead after their resurrection and appearance at the final judgment: just as in the gospels where we read that "the *dead* man ὁ νεκρὸς *sat up* and *began to speak*," Luke vii. 15, "the *deaf hear*," Matt. xi. 5, "the *dumb* man ὁ κωφὸς *spake*," Matt. ix. 33, and in Matt. xv. 31, "they saw . . . the *lame* to *walk* and the *blind* to *see*," the epithets *dead*, *deaf*, *dumb*, *lame*, *blind*, identify the persons spoken of; but no one supposes that they continued dead, deaf, dumb, lame, and blind after the miracles had been performed. So with regard to the dead here spoken of, they were "*dead*" persons *before* their resurrection, not after it. The risen dead here symbolize persons raised from a state of death at the epoch denoted, there being no other symbol which could properly represent them. The scenic representation, therefore, of a real, corporeal resurrection is exhibited in the vision, because there is no other symbolization, no analogous change of men or other beings, which could adequately foreshow such an event. The transition of a chrysalis into a winged insect, for example, beautiful as it may be for an illustration, would have been utterly insufficient as a prophetic symbol of the stupendous change which is to take place in the resurrection. The former is but the passage from one state of bodily *life* to another: the latter is to be a re-animation from a state of bodily *death*. The analogy, therefore, would have failed in the very thing to be foreshown.

In like manner in verse fourth (Rev. xx.) where the resurrection of the righteous is symbolized, the beloved disciple speaks of the souls of those who had been beheaded, &c., and says "they lived and reigned with Christ a thousand years," or rather, according to the reading of the best editions, τὰ χίλια ἔτη, "*the* thousand years," that is, those which had been mentioned in verse third as indicating the period of Satan's confinement in the abyss. He calls them *souls*, to identify them as those who having been departed spirits were to have their portion, at the epoch denoted by the vision, in the resurrection to immortal glory. This is evident from the fact mentioned that this class of the dead, *the blessed and holy*, "lived" at the beginning of the thousand years and reigned with Christ during that whole period, whereas "*the rest of the dead*"—that is, those who at that epoch had already died without being in the number of "the blessed and holy"—"LIVED NOT AGAIN until the thousand years were finished," verses 4, 5. The one class were raised previous to "the thousand years:" the other not till after the expiration of that period. Both classes were disembodied *souls* and *dead* persons before their resurrection, not after it: and hence as these epithets are used as marks of identity in the two cases, the word *souls* presents no more objection to the real literal resurrection of the one class, than the word *dead* does to that of the other class. When it is said that the souls of the martyrs "*lived*" at the epoch referred to, the meaning cannot be that their disembodied spirits had no conscious existence during the previous period which had elapsed since the death of their bodies: for that is contrary to the symbolization under the fifth seal in Rev. vi. 9–11, where they are represented as having such an existence, and are enjoined to wait patiently until their number should be complete, when they were to be avenged upon their enemies. It cannot mean that these departed souls were then to have a spiritual resurrection from a death in trespasses and sins, for no such change takes place after death: neither was it any more necessary in their case, for they were "*the blessed and holy*," and hence had been already regenerated. It cannot denote that the martyr spirit was to revive during the millennium, for living agents denote living agents, and not mere acts and states either of body or mind. Besides, the martyr spirit is an enduring patient disposition in the midst of trials and persecution: but there will be no opportunity for the exercise of any such spirit during the millennium. It is conceded that men in general, if not universally, will at that epoch be holy. Public opinion will then be as strong against persecution for righteousness' sake, as it ever was in its favor. The persecuting civil and ecclesiastical rulers denoted by the wild beast and the false prophet will have been cast into the place of punishment symbolized by the lake of fire, Rev. xix. 20. The organized confederacy against Christ will have been completely overthrown. Rev. xix. 11–21. The fallen angels symbolized by Satan their chief, Rev. xx. 2, 3, will have been shut up in the place denoted by "the bottomless pit," "that they should deceive the nations no more, till the thousand years should be fulfilled," Rev. xx. 3. Neither men nor devils can disturb the saints during the period foreshown. It is a time of triumph and rejoicing, not of endurance and suffering. How then can there be any room for the exercise of the martyr spirit? It will not do to say that the martyr spirit is a holy disposition, for such a disposition is not by any means confined to the martyrs, but is the common characteristic of all the righteous. The martyr spirit is not simply a holy disposition, but such a disposition exercised under circumstances of trial, suffering, and persecution.

There is but one other meaning that the word "*lived*" can have as here used, and that is, that the souls of the righteous lived again in union with their bodies, though, as we learn from other passages, those bodies will be in a glorified condition, like the risen body of our Lord Jesus Christ. This word therefore implies a real, corporeal resurrection at the epoch denoted by the vision.

This is demonstrably evident from the fact that the blessed and holy who had part in the first resurrection are in the context contrasted with the rest of the dead who lived not again, that is, who did not rise from a state of death till after the thousand years had expired. We have an account of that resurrection in verse twelfth, which, as we have already shown, manifestly denotes a *real* and literal resurrection. The whole collective mass of the dead are divided into two parts—"the blessed and holy" whose portion is in "the first resurrection"—these are *one part:* the *other* part have their portion in the last resurrection. As the latter is real, so the former must be real also. As the resurrection at the end of the thousand years is a literal resurrection, so also is that at the beginning of the thousand years.

But further, there is no express explanation of the symbolic vision respecting the former, namely the post-millennial resurrection. We are left to deduce that resurrection from the context and the symbolization: and that a real resurrection is foreshown, is undeniably true. It is, however, a matter of inference: whereas in regard to the other symbolization contained in verse fourth, namely, that of the pre-millennial resurrection, we have the inspired explanation—"THIS IS,"—in other words, this symbolization denotes, or this scenic representation is the symbol of "THE FIRST RESURRECTION," Rev. xx. 5.

That such is the true meaning of that verse is demonstrable from the invariable usage of the sacred writers in the inspired interpretation of symbols. Thus when the risen Saviour says—"the seven stars are the messengers of the churches: and the seven candlesticks which thou sawest are the seven churches," Rev. i. 20, the meaning evidently is that those symbolic stars DENOTE or REPRESENT those messengers, and that those symbolic candlesticks DENOTE or REPRESENT those churches. When it is said in Rev. xvii. 15—"the waters which thou sawest where the harlot sitteth are peoples, and multitudes, and nations, and tongues," the meaning clearly is, that those symbolic waters DENOTE or REPRESENT vast multitudes of different nations speaking different languages. When it is said in Dan vii. 17, "these great beasts which are four are four kings," the meaning is that these beasts DENOTE or REPRESENT or *are the symbols of* four kings, that is, four ruling dynasties. When it is said in Dan. viii. 20, 21, that "the ram which thou sawest having two horns are the kings of Media and Persia, and the rough goat is the king of Grecia, and the great horn that is between his eyes is the first king," the meaning confessedly is, that the ram DENOTES or REPRESENTS the Medo-

Persian dynasty; and the goat, the Grecian; and the great horn, the first dynasty among the victorious Grecians. In these inspired interpretations, and so in all the others in the Scriptures, wherever it is said that a given symbol such as a candlestick, a ram, a wild beast, &c., IS any given thing, the meaning invariably is, DENOTES or REPRESENTS such a thing. The verb *to be* is commonly expressed, as in Rev. i. 20, where it occurs in the form of the third person plural present indicative—in the Greek εἰσί, and in English "*are.*" In Rev. xx. 5, the same verb or its equivalent is understood,—Αὕτη ἡ ἀνάστασις ἡ πρωτη, literally translated—"THIS, THE RESURRECTION THE FIRST," the verb ἔστιν, *is*, being implied. The invariable usage of Scripture, therefore, demonstrates that the correct exposition of the words is—"THIS," *i. e. this symbolization* just described in verse fourth, to which verse we must look as embodying the antecedent of the pronoun αὕτη THIS—*this symbolization* or *representation* denotes or foreshows THE FIRST RESURRECTION.* The word *resurrection*, therefore, is an inspired interpretation of something that was symbolized in the vision, and hence it must be

* Lord's Review of Brown. Theol. and Lit. Journal for July, 1851.

taken in its literal import: for such is the usage of Scripture. To recur to the examples just cited:—when the seven candlesticks are explained as symbolizing seven churches, or congregations of visible worshippers; the meaning is *literal congregations of real men*, not something which such congregations metaphorically resemble. When the waters are explained as symbolizing vast multitudes of nations speaking different languages, *real literal nations* and *real literal languages* are obviously intended. When the ram is explained as symbolizing the Medo-Persian dynasty, a *real dynasty*, and not a figurative one, is signified. Agreeably to this usage, therefore, the word *resurrection*, which is here employed as an inspired interpretation of something symbolized in the vision, must denote a literal and not a figurative resurrection. Nothing, therefore, can be more demonstrably certain than that the Scriptures teach that there will be A LITERAL RESURRECTION OF BELIEVERS*

* Professor Stuart, who was a strenuous anti-millenarian, fully admits that this is a *real* and *literal* resurrection. He says that he does not see how we can fairly avoid such a conclusion, and that he has "given reasons why we seem to be constrained to admit the sense of a *bodily* resurrection like to the last and final one."—*Stuart on the Apocalypse*, vol. ii. Excursus vi. p. 476.

antecedent to the period denoted by "the thousand years," commonly called the millennium or age of millennial blessedness, when the earth is to be full of the knowledge of the Lord as the waters cover the sea, and when Christ and his glorified saints are to extend their beneficent sway over all peoples, nations, and languages under the whole heaven.

In a word, St. John saw in vision a collection of the symbolic risen dead sitting upon thrones, which foreshows that those whom they represented were, at the epoch denoted by the vision, to be invested with regal authority—this collection of persons doubtless symbolizing the whole number of the deceased righteous at the epoch indicated: and among this glorious throng which he beheld he mentions two classes in particular that attracted his attention. One was the martyrs: the other, those who, without suffering martyrdom, had not yielded an idolatrous homage to the persons symbolized by the beast.

"And I saw thrones, and they sat upon them, and judgment was given unto them," that is, those who sat upon the thrones were invested with authority to act as judges: "and I saw the souls of them that were beheaded for the witness of Jesus and for the word of God, and οἵτινες whoever had not worshipped the beast, neither his image, neither had received his mark upon their foreheads, or in their hands: and they lived and reigned with Christ τὰ χίλια ἔτη the thousand years. But the rest of the dead lived not again until the thousand years were finished. THIS IS THE FIRST RESURRECTION. Blessed and holy is he that hath part in the first resurrection: on such the second death hath no power, but they shall be priests of God and of Christ, and shall reign with him a thousand years." Rev. xx. 4–6.

The vision, therefore, denotes a real, literal resurrection antecedent to the millennium; and when it is said that the blessed and holy have part in that resurrection, and that on such the second death hath no power, the design is to teach us that none but such as are blessed and holy rise to a life of immortal glory, and become exempt from the fearful doom which is in store for the wicked.

The symbolic risen saints seen in the vision, Rev. xx. 4, represent the real saints, the blessed and holy, that are to be raised at Christ's coming; their resurrection foreshows the real resurrection of the saints at that epoch; their investiture with judicial power and regal authority, the similar investiture of the saints whom they symbolize: and in every instance in the sacred Scriptures where a symbol is of the *same* species with that which is symbolized, there is a reason for such a symbolization in the nature of the case, inasmuch as to have used a symbol of a *different* species would have involved an incongruity, and have failed of its object.

We have thus proved the truth of the third law of symbolization by the same line of argument as that adopted in regard to the first and second, namely, by an appeal to the word of God, and the interpretations either directly given therein or legitimately inferred from the context. We have proved it by the vision in Rev. v., where the incarnate Son of God, the Lord Jesus Christ, the risen and divine Redeemer, appears in person as the Lamb whom saints and angels worship; and by the vision in Rev. xix. where the celestial Leader who is followed by the armies from heaven is expressly styled "THE WORD OF GOD, KING *of kings and* LORD *of lords*." We have proved it also by the vision in Rev. iv. where God the Father appears as his own representative; by the white-robed palm-bearers, Rev. vii.; by the spirits of the martyrs under the fifth seal, Rev. vi.; by the men who hid themselves from the wrath of *the Lamb*, Rev. vi.; by the two witnesses, Rev. xi.; by the servants of Christ, Rev. xii., who are spoken of as overcoming by the blood of *the Lamb* and as loving not their lives unto the death; by the men who worshipped the beast, Rev. xiii.; by the men who repented not of their idolatries and other sins, Rev. ix.; by the men who blasphemed the name of God and persevered in impenitence, Rev. xvi.; by the kings of the whole world, Rev. xvi. 14, 16; by Satan and the angel who confined him, Rev. xx. 1–3; by the unholy raised from death, Rev. xx. 12, 13, 15; and by the enthroned saints representing the "blessed and holy" who, in "the first resurrection," are to be raised from the dead to reign with Christ during the period symbolized by the thousand years, Rev. xx. 4–6.

Such a multitude of passages demonstrating the truth of this law must therefore be considered as fully establishing the principle, as one revealed in the word of God, that *symbols that are of such a nature, station, or relation, that there is nothing of an analogous kind that they can represent, symbolize agents, objects, acts, or events of their own kind.*

CHAPTER VI.

DISCUSSION OF THE FOURTH LAW.

IV. "THE FOURTH LAW: *When the symbol and that which it symbolizes differ from each other, the correspondence between the representative and that which it represents, still extends to their chief parts; and the general elements or parts of the symbol denote corresponding parts in that which is symbolized.*"

Here also the Scriptures furnish the most abundant proof. Thus, while the victorious ram, in its successful pushing against other beasts, denoted a conquering dynasty, its two horns indicated that the dynasty was complex, which was historically verified in the Medo-Persian. Dan. viii. 4, 20. The inspired explanation is—"*The ram which thou sawest having two horns are the kings of Media and Persia.*" This is exactly what has been stated in the law under consideration, namely, that, in the circumstances specified, the chief parts of the symbol have a corresponding reality in that which is symbolized.

In like manner, when the ram was afterwards overthrown by the he-goat, the symbolization foreshowed that the dynasty represented by the ram would be subverted by that which was represented by the goat, in other words the Medo-Persian by the Grecian. The fact that the "he-goat came from the west on the face of the whole earth and touched not the ground," indicated that the conqueror was to come from that direction, and advance with great rapidity in his career of triumph. Dan. viii. 5. The large horn between his eyes denoted, according to the inspired interpretation, verse 21, "the first king," to wit, Alexander the Great who conquered Darius. The horn in its broken state foreshowed a corresponding condition of the dynasty symbolized: and the springing up of four horns in its place, verse 8, indicated, according to the inspired interpretation, verse 22, that four dynasties were to arise who should divide among themselves the empire of their former chief. All this was historically fulfilled. The regal sway was not perpetuated in the family of Alexander: their reign lasted only for a short period after his death, and was little more than nominal: and at length four of his generals, distributing the empire among themselves, reigned each in his own quarter, as the successors of their illustrious master. Here, too, we see the law verified in the fact that there is a correspondence between the different parts of the symbol and that which it represents.

So also the several parts of the great image seen by Nebuchadnezzar in his dream had their corresponding realities in the agents symbolized. The head of gold, Dan. ii. 32, represented, according to the inspired interpretation, the Babylonian dynasty: "Thou, O king . . . thou art this head of gold," verses 37, 38. The breasts and arms of silver, verse 32, denoted, according to the inspired interpretation, verse 39, another dynasty which was to succeed the Babylonian, and that *second* dynasty, we know from history, was the Medo-Persian. The belly and thighs of brass, verse 32, represented according to the inspired interpretation, verse 39, a *third* dynasty which was to succeed the second, and that third dynasty, we know from history, was the Grecian. The legs of iron and the feet part of iron and part of clay (that is, according to the meaning of the original, *burnt clay* or *potters' ware*), verse 33, denoted, according to the inspired interpretation, verse 40, a *fourth* dynasty, and that, we know from history, was the Roman which succeeded the Grecian or third dynasty in this series. The strength of the iron indicated an analogous element in the rulers of the fourth great monarchy. The brittleness of the clay or potters'-ware, on the other hand, foreshowed an element corresponding to that symbol, verses 41, 42. The want of thorough union between the iron and clay denoted, according to the inspired interpretation, verse 43, an analogous want of union between the strong and the fragile elements, that is, as verified in history, between the powerful monarchs or chief rulers and the people —"the seed of men"—admitted to a share in the government by means of the elective franchise. The crushing of the image by the stone, verses 34, 35, denoted, according to the inspired interpretation, verse 44, that the dynasties symbolized by the image were to be destroyed by that symbolized by the stone.* What stronger

* The dream with the inspired interpretation is as follows: Dan. ii. 31–45.

Verse 31. "Thou, O king, sawest and behold a great image. This great image, whose brightness was excellent, stood before thee; and the form thereof was terrible.

32. This image's *head* was of fine *gold*, his *breast* and his *arms* of *silver*, his *belly* and his *thighs* of *brass*.

33. His *legs* of *iron*, his *feet* part of *iron* and part of *clay*.

34. Thou sawest till that a *stone* was cut out without hands,

proof could we have of the truth of our fourth law that there is such a correspondence, as we

which *smote the image upon his feet that were of iron and clay, and brake them to pieces.*

35. Then was the iron, the clay, the brass, the silver, and the gold, *broken to pieces* together, and became like the chaff of the summer threshing-floors; and the wind carried them away, that no place was found for them: and *the stone* that smote the image *became a great mountain, and filled the whole earth.*

36. This is THE DREAM; and we will tell THE INTERPRETATION thereof before the king.

37. *Thou, O king,* art a king of kings: for the God of heaven hath given thee a kingdom, power, and strength, and glory.

38. And wheresoever the children of men dwell, the beasts of the field and the fowls of the heaven hath he given into thine hand, and hath made thee ruler over them all. *Thou art this head of gold.*

39. And after thee shall arise *another* kingdom inferior to thee, and another *third* kingdom of brass which shall bear rule over all the earth.

40. And the *fourth* kingdom shall be *strong as iron:* forasmuch as iron breaketh in pieces and subdueth all things: and as iron that breaketh all these, shall it break in pieces and bruise.

41. And whereas thou sawest the feet and toes, part of potters'-clay, and part of iron, *the kingdom shall be divided;* but there shall be in it of *the strength of the iron,* forasmuch as thou sawest the iron mixed with miry clay.

42. And as the toes of the feet were *part of iron* and *part of clay,* so the kingdom shall be *partly strong* and *partly broken* (brittle or fragile).

have stated, between the chief parts of the symbol and that which the symbol represents? *The inspired interpretations*, as we have seen, demonstrate the correctness of that law, and this demonstration is confirmed by acknowledged historical facts. What further proof could be desired? Or what more conclusive line of argument could be adopted in this discussion? *The main point at issue is whether these laws are sustained by the inspired interpretations:* and we are proving that they are, by pointing out *the exact agreement between the one and the other.*

But conclusive as are the facts already presented, there is additional evidence to which we would briefly call the attention of the reader.

43. And whereas thou sawest iron mixed with miry clay, they shall mingle themselves with the seed of men: but *they shall not cleave one to another, even as iron is not mixed with clay.*

44. *And in the days of these kings shall the God of heaven set up a kingdom which shall never be destroyed: and the kingdom shall not be left to other people, but* IT SHALL BREAK IN PIECES AND CONSUME ALL THESE KINGDOMS, *and it shall stand for ever.*

45. Forasmuch as thou sawest that the stone was cut out of the mountain without hands, and that it brake in pieces the iron, the brass, the clay, the silver, and the gold; *the great God hath made known to the king what shall come to pass hereafter:* and *the dream is certain, and the interpretation thereof sure.*"

In the parallel vision* in Dan. vii., the rulers of the four great empires were symbolized by

* The four great empires in each case, Dan. ii. 31–45, and vii. 3–27, cover the whole period from the time of Nebuchadnezzar to the establishment of the kingdom of Christ and his saints. In Dan. vii. 17, "These great beasts, which are four, are four kings which shall arise out of the earth;" the future tense in the verb "*shall arise*," is used in speaking of these dynasties as a whole, because three out of four were then future. Commentators are generally agreed that the four empires whose rulers are symbolized by the great image in Dan. ii., are the same with those whose rulers are represented by the four beasts in Dan. vii.

The only universal monarchy immediately succeeding the Babylonian, the Medo-Persian, and the Grecian, and answering to the description in Dan. vii. 7–23, as a fierce and all-conquering power, was THE ROMAN, and therefore the fourth or ten-horned beast must symbolize the supreme and subordinate rulers of that empire.

Professor Stuart maintains (Commentary on Daniel, p. 202), that the fourth beast symbolizes "the four kingdoms of Alexander's successors." But the dynasties of Alexander's generals were merely a part of the series or line of rulers symbolized by the winged leopard with four heads, or *third* beast of Dan. vii. 6, and by the he-goat with a great horn, in place of which came up four other horns, Dan. viii. 8. They cannot, therefore, be denoted by the *fourth* beast, which was altogether separate from the *third*, and represented an entirely distinct line of rulers.

The ten-horned beast, in Dan. vii., symbolizes the rulers of the Western Roman Empire in its different stages down to its final overthrow, when Christ's kingdom is to be established four ravenous beasts. The first beast, like the head of gold, represented the first or Babylonian

We say the *Western* Roman Empire, because that division of the Empire was the one which was distinct in its appropriate territories from those which were governed by the dynasties represented by the first three beasts; and the kingdoms in modern Europe which occupy the territorial platform of the Western Empire, are in the view of the Holy Spirit essentially that same empire, just as the "ten kings" denote, not merely the original chiefs of the primary ten kingdoms, but also their successors in the sovereign rule. It is from overlooking this fact that Professor Stuart has been unable to see how the fourth beast, in the seventh chapter of Daniel, can symbolize the rulers of the Roman Empire, inasmuch as he cannot discover in that empire any element corresponding to the clay of the great image, prior to "the conquest by Goths and Vandals, and the subsequent division of the empire." "A more compact, undivided, powerful dynasty," he adds, "never arose on earth" (Commentary on Daniel, p. 193). But such characteristics correspond exactly with the "legs of iron," Dan. ii. 33. It is to a later period that we must look for an element of weakness corresponding to the clay that was mingled with the iron in the ten toes. That we are not coining imaginary facts to sustain a preconceived hypothesis, is evident from the language of the celebrated historian, who had no belief in the inspiration of the prophecies, and who speaks of *the Western Empire* as having, after its previous decay, a renewed existence in the time of Charlemagne (Gibbon's Rome, chapter xlix.). This shows that Gibbon perceived part of the truth, though he came far short of what is made known to the discerning Christian in the revelation of God's word. How strikingly in our own day have the kingdoms of Western and dynasty; the second beast, like the breasts and arms of silver, the second or Medo-Persian dynasty; the third beast, like the belly and thighs of brass, the third or Grecian dynasty; the fourth beast, like the legs of iron, and the feet part of iron, and part of clay, Dan. ii. 33, 42, the fourth or Roman dynasty, Dan. vii. 17, 23; the ten horns of this beast, like the ten toes of the great image, the "ten kings," or supreme civil rulers

South Western Europe exhibited in their rulers and people what was foreshown by the prophecy, the mingled characteristics of iron and clay! As the rulers symbolized by the ten-horned beast bear sway until the epoch when Christ and the saints (who, as we shall hereafter show, are not persons in the "natural body," but those in the glorified or "spiritual body") are to be invested with the dominion over all peoples, nations, and languages under the whole heaven, Dan. vii. 9–18, 21, 22, 26, 27, the empire over which they (the rulers denoted by the fourth beast) reign must be considered as essentially the same empire down to that period; and as the third beast, in Dan. vii., represented the line of *Grecian* rulers, commencing with Alexander the Great, and continued in his successors, and the fourth beast, *a series of rulers, which commenced the next in point of time to the Grecian*, and was to have dominion until the period for the setting up of the kingdom of Christ and the saints over all nations, the succession denoted by the fourth beast had its historical counterpart in the *Roman* dynasties: and these indubitable facts overturn the opinion of the Futurists, who hold that the fourth beast denotes, exclusively, a persecuting power which has not yet appeared.

of the ten kingdoms,* Dan. vii. 24; and the little horn (which was the eleventh, and to make way for the growth of which three of the other horns were plucked up), a line of rulers who were to be diverse from the others, Dan. vii. 8, 24.

Here, too, we see the same indications of correspondence between the chief parts of the symbol and that which it represents; and the inspired interpretations in verses 17, 23, 24 (Dan. vii.), respecting the four great beasts and the ten horns, and the little horn of the fourth beast, fully sustain the law.

We might strengthen the argument in support of this fourth law, by referring to the "seven heads" which appeared on the apocalyptic dragon and wild beast, Rev. xii. xiii. xvii.

Without entering, however, into the historical exposition, it will be sufficient for our present purpose to remind the reader that the "seven heads" which were parts of the complex symbol, denote, according to the inspired interpretation, "seven kings," Rev. xvii. 10, that is, seven lines or successions of chiefs or rulers having the supreme authority, of whom five had already passed away when St. John saw the vision,

* Those into which the Western Empire was divided by the irruptions of the Goths, Vandals, and other barbarous tribes.

and one (the sixth in the series) was then in existence.* And what is this inspired interpre-

* "And here is the mind which hath wisdom, the *seven heads* are seven mountains at (Gr. ἐπι followed by a genitive) which the woman sitteth. And there are *seven kings;* five are fallen, and one is, and the other is not yet come; and when he cometh, he must continue a short space," Rev. xvii. 9, 10. When it is said, that "the seven heads are seven mountains," or hills, "and there are seven kings," the meaning is, that the *seven heads* and the seven hills (which were probably the seven hills of Rome seen in vision) symbolize the same persons, that is, *seven kings*, or seven lines of chief magistrates, or supreme rulers; just as the two witnesses represent the same persons as might be symbolized by two olive trees and two candlesticks, Rev. xi. 3, 4. Nearly all the commentators, however, have interpreted *the seven heads as symbolizing not only the seven kings, but also the seven hills*, which is absurd; for if the *seven hills*, as well as the *seven kings*, or lines of chiefs, are symbolized by the *seven heads*, then as these "*kings*" were not contemporaneous, neither could the hills be. So also, in Rev. xvii. 18, the meaning is not that the woman, who was seen riding on a ten-horned beast, was a symbol of the city of Rome, but that this "*woman*," whose name was "*Babylon the Great*," Rev. xvii. 5, symbolized the same class of persons as the "*great city*" *Babylon* symbolized, which is repeatedly spoken of in the Apocalypse under the appellation of the "*great city*," and "*great Babylon*," Rev. xiv. 8; xvi. 19; xviii. 2, 10, 18, 19, 21, and which, *as a symbol city*—"the great city having dominion, ἔχουσα βασιλείαν, over the kings of the earth," Rev. xvii. 18—had been exhibited to St. John in the visions in which he saw the Euphrates flowing through it, Rev. xvi. 12, and the city divided into three parts, verse 19.

tation but another statement of our fourth law of prophetic symbols that, in the circumstances specified in that law, there is a correspondence between the chief parts of the symbol and that which is symbolized.

So, also, the "ten horns" of the apocalyptic wild beast, like the ten which were seen by Daniel, are explained in the inspired interpretation to mean "ten kings," rulers or governors, Rev. xvii. 12. Here, too, is another correspondence like that above mentioned, and an additional proof of the correctness of the law.

The same is true also, of the woman who rode upon the beast. This harlot sorceress, who is styled "Babylon the Great," Rev. xvii. 5, is exhibited, Rev. xvii. 3, as sitting *upon* (Gr. ἐπι followed by the accusative case) a seven-headed and ten-horned wild beast. She is said, Rev. xvii. 1, to sit *at* (Gr. ἐπι followed by the genitive) the many waters which, in verse 15th, are explained as symbolizing "peoples, and multitudes, and nations, and tongues," that is,* great

* In another vision, Rev. xiii. 4, the masses of the people (which are symbolized in Rev. xvii., by the waters at which the woman was sitting) are exhibited as worshipping the beast. The body of the people, therefore, are not represented by the body of the beast, for that would be to confound

masses of people of different nations and languages, making in the aggregate a dense multitude, analogous to a vast collection of waters. The woman does not symbolize the civil rulers of the ten kingdoms, for they are represented by the seven-headed and ten-horned wild beast which carries and supports her. She does not symbolize the great body of the people composing a church, or collection of churches, for the masses of the people are symbolized by the waters at which the woman sitteth. She must therefore represent *an organized body of ecclesiastical rulers and teachers, as they are the only class that is not comprised in the civil rulers and common people.* She was "arrayed in purple and scarlet color, and decked with gold and precious stones and pearls," Rev. xvii. 4. Her jewels and clothing represent the wealth, luxury, and pomp of the persons symbolized. She had "a golden cup in her hand

the object worshipped with those who worship. The beast is one thing, those who worship it another. In Rev. xiii. 4, agreeably to our third law, the people, for reasons already assigned, are represented by those of their own species; and as the body and inferior parts of the beast do not symbolize the great masses of the people, they must, as distinguished from the heads and horns, denote the *subordinate* rulers and magistrates.

full of abominations and filthiness of her fornication." This indicates that those whom she represents have the disposition to entice others to idolatry and apostasy. "Upon her forehead was a name written, Mystery, Babylon the Great, the Mother of harlots, and abominations of the earth," Rev. xvii. 5, which foreshows that the character of those symbolized would be that of persons exerting an artful and successful agency in the seduction of others, and constituting an organized structure of men analogous to that of a great city like Babylon. She was "drunken with the blood of the saints, and with the blood of the martyrs* of Jesus," Rev. xvii. 6, which denotes that the persons here symbolized were to become intoxicated with joy from persecuting, even unto death, the people of God.

But, without swelling this Essay into a large volume, by gathering together the almost innumerable proofs which we find upon the pages of Scripture, the evidence already presented is abundantly sufficient to show, in regard to this fourth law of symbolization, that when the symbol is of a different order from the thing symbolized, the resemblance extends to their chief

* In the Greek, τῶν μαρτύρων, the *witnesses* the same word as in Rev. xi. 3.

parts, and the general elements in the one correspond to the general elements in the other. The two horns of the ram; the great horn of the he-goat; the four horns which grew up after that horn was broken; the various characteristics, acts, and relations exhibited in the scenic representation of these symbol animals; the several parts of the great image; the ten horns, and the eleventh or little horn of the fourth beast; the seven heads and ten horns of the apocalyptic dragon and wild beast; and the harlot sorceress, with her gorgeous attire, her conspicuous name, and her golden cup—all have their counterpart in corresponding realities: and the same is true of all the interpreted symbols. The law, therefore, may be considered as having the most ample demonstration.

CHAPTER VII.

Discussion of the fifth law

V. "The Fifth Law: *The Names of Symbols are their Literal and Proper Names.*"

Thus, as is evident from what was said in the discussion of the third law, such denominatives as "*the Lamb,*" "*the Word of God,*" "*the Lion of the tribe of Judah,*" "*the Root of David,*" Rev. v. and xix., are used in the Apocalypse as proper names of the Son of God. The person indicated by these titles is Jehovah-Jesus, God manifest in the flesh; and, in his risen and glorified humanity, he appears in vision to the beloved disciple.

Again, when it is said that John saw seven candlesticks, seven stars, seven heads, ten horns, a great red dragon, diadems on the heads or on the horns, a woman sitting upon* a beast, and at† the many waters, a beautiful city adorned with precious stones, and so in all other similar

* Gr. ἐπι followed by an accusative.

† Gr ἐπι followed by a genitive.

cases, the language is, in every instance, literally descriptive of what was seen in the vision. So in the account of the different parts of the great image, Dan. ii., the words *iron*, *clay*, *brass*, *silver*, *gold*, are all used in their literal sense, and tell us exactly what Nebuchadnezzar saw in his dream. As there is no end to the objects which resemble candlesticks, stars, cities, rams, he-goats, heads, horns, iron, clay, &c., and might be called such by a metaphor, if the terms used in describing the symbols be not their literal and proper names, we could not tell what the symbols were; we should find ourselves on a sea of conjecture, and, except where we had an inspired explanation, there would be an end to everything like demonstrative, or even probable interpretation.

It is in vain to say that we could be certain of the meaning when the prophecy was fulfilled: for we could not tell whether a symbolic prophecy was fulfilled in any given event, or that a symbolic agent was verified in any given person or class of persons, unless we could first tell what the symbol was. How could we otherwise perceive any analogy or correspondence between the symbol and that which it represented? As well might we say that a given object resembled a cube, or a sphere, or a pyramid, or a cylinder, or that a given figure was like a square, or a circle, or a triangle, or a parallelogram, when we had no conception of the meaning of such terms.

The names of symbols, therefore, are their literal and proper names.

CHAPTER VIII.

Discussion of the sixth law.

VI. "The Sixth Law: *A Single Agent, in many instances, symbolizes a Body and Succession of Agents.*"

Thus, the fourth or ten-horned beast of Daniel, which, as a symbol, was a single agent, represented a body or collection of agents, namely, the rulers of the Roman Empire. It symbolized the power which was to succeed the Grecian dynasty represented by the third beast, and to bear sway over the earth, Dan. vii. 23; and that power was undeniably the Roman. It also denoted a succession of agents, for it is described as acting until the coming of the Ancient of Days, and the possession of the kingdom by the saints of the Most High, Dan. vii. 9–22, a period which is yet future.*

In like manner, the first three beasts, in Dan. vii., each symbolized a collection and succession of agents, namely, the rulers of the

* See above, Note, pp. 84–86.

Babylonian, Medo-Persian, and Grecian monarchies.

A candlestick, as we have seen, symbolizes an assembly of visible worshippers; the seven candlesticks symbolized the seven churches of Asia; and each of those churches comprised a number of individuals, and also a succession of individuals, so long as the churches existed.

The ram with its two horns, and the he-goat with its great horn, in place of which grew up four horns, Dan. viii., symbolized a body and succession of agents; the former, the Medo-Persian; the latter, the dynasty of Alexander and his generals.

The two witnesses, Rev. xi., symbolize certain faithful churches and their ministers,* who testify for Christ throughout the specified career of those denoted by the beast from the sea, Rev. xi. 3, compared with xiii. 5; and consequently, they represent a body and succession of agents.

We might give additional proof of the truth of this law by a reference to other symbols; but these are sufficient for its verification.

A single agent, therefore, *in many instances, symbolizes a body and succession of agents.*

* See above, chapter v., pp. 52–58.

CHAPTER IX.

Discussion of the seventh law.

VII. The Seventh Law: *The periods of time during which a representative agent performs certain representative acts, symbolize the periods during which the agents denoted by the symbols perform the corresponding acts; and in all those cases where such an interpretation is not contrary to analogy, days symbolize years.*

If agents denote agents, and acts denote acts, then the periods during which symbolical agents perform a given symbolical agency must foreshow the periods during which the agents denoted by the symbols perform the corresponding acts.

Thus, when Ezekiel, as a symbol of the house of Israel, lay upon his left side three hundred and ninety days, it foreshadowed an analogous period in reference to Israel. When, as a symbol of the house of Judah, he lay upon his right side forty days, it foreshowed an analogous period in reference to Judah. The inspired explanation is—"I have appointed thee *each day for a year*," Ezek. iv. 6. The three hundred and ninety days, therefore, symbolized three hundred and ninety years; and the forty days, forty years; and this is according to analogy. The shorter period of a day in which the earth performs a revolution on its axis, is evidently fitted to symbolize the longer period of an astronomical or solar year in which the earth performs a revolution round the sun. And that the years denoted are solar, and not lunar years, is corroborated by the fact, that while on the one hand the Jewish months were lunar, being reckoned from one new moon to another, their *years* were always *solar*, being reckoned from equinox to equinox, their civil year from the autumnal equinox, and their sacred year from the vernal; and as they counted but twelve months to the year, and these months were lunar, in order to make up the deficiency they inserted, every three years, an intercalary month called Veadar, that is, the second Adar. In the Apocalypse twelve months are reckoned, in round numbers, to the year, and thirty days to the month, or three hundred and sixty days to the year; as is evident from the expressions, forty-two months, twelve hundred and sixty days, and time, times, and half a time, or three years and a half, which are used interchangeably.* In converting years, therefore, in the symbolic prophecies into the equivalent expression in days, three hundred and sixty days must be reckoned to the year; but *each of those days*, in its symbolical import, must be considered as representing *a full revolution of the earth round the sun*, for this is required by analogy, that is, *a complete astronomical* or *solar year* from equinox to equinox. Consequently, according to the apocalyptic usage, the equivalent expression for one thousand years, Rev. xx., would be three hundred and sixty thousand days; and these days, according to the law which we are considering, would represent three hundred and sixty thousand astronomical or solar years.

The inspired explanation in Ezek. iv. 6—"I have appointed thee *each day for a year*"—shows what is meant *in all cases of the same class;* in other words, that in all cases where the agency is symbolic, and *the symbolic period measuring that agency* is expressed in *days* or their

* Months. 42 × Days. 30 = Days. 1260—Rev. xi. 2, 3; xiii. 5; and
Years. 3½ × Days. 360 = Days. 1260—Rev. xii. 6, 14; and
Years. 3½ × Months. 12 = Months 42.

equivalent, "*each day*" represents "*a year*," provided that in the particular example to which the principle is applied, there be nothing contrary to analogy in such an interpretation.

If a succession of rulers be symbolized by a wild beast, it is quite according to analogy that the beast on the one hand should be represented as acting for twelve hundred and sixty *days*, for that period does not exceed the ordinary life of a beast; and on the other hand, as it respects the series of rulers, that *each day* should symbolize *a year*, for it is not contrary to the nature either of a civil or an ecclesiastical dynasty that it should continue for twelve hundred and sixty *years*.

Thus, in Rev. xiii., the ten-horned wild beast is *a symbol; his agency is symbolic; and, therefore, the period which measures that agency is also symbolic*, and as there is nothing in this case contrary to analogy in such an interpretation, the twelve hundred and sixty *days* in which the beast exerts his agency, symbolize the twelve hundred and sixty *years* in which the succession of civil rulers denoted by the beast exert their corresponding and analogous agency. These rulers have already exerted for more than twelve hundred years the agency foreshown; and that undeniable historical fact establishes the correctness of the principle.

Similar remarks apply to this period in its relation to the "two witnesses," Rev. xi. It is not contrary to analogy that for twelve hundred and sixty *days*, two individual men should continue faithful to the truth; or on the other hand, that for twelve hundred and sixty *years* there should be a succession of faithful ministers and people, constituting the symbolized churches and pastors. That prophecy, therefore, foreshowed that those who are represented by the witnesses were to testify for Jesus through a period of this duration.

It has already been shown that there will be a real resurrection of the saints anterior to the millennium, and that the equivalent expression for one thousand years, Rev. xx. 2–7, is three hundred and sixty thousand days. As it is not incompatible with the nature of Satan that he should be imprisoned for three hundred and sixty thousand years, or with the nature of glorified and immortal saints, that they should reign with Christ during the same period; and as the act of the angel, in the vision, in laying hold upon Satan and shutting him up, is a symbolical act, and consequently the period which measures the duration of his imprisonment a symbolical period, it follows that the principle of "*a day for a year*" must be applied here also, and that the three hundred and sixty thousand days symbolize *three hundred and sixty thousand astronomical or solar years.*

It has been objected to these views, that the seven times of Nebuchadnezzar's insanity, Dan. iv., cannot denote two thousand five hundred and twenty years, that being the product of seven multiplied by three hundred and sixty. But how does that affect this law of prophetic symbols? The *seven times*, in Dan. iv. 16, are not predicated of the symbol, but of the person symbolized; and therefore the objection is of no force against the law in question. This is demonstrably the fact from what is said in that passage—"*let his heart be changed from man's, and let a beast's heart be given him*, and let *seven times* pass over HIM." A man's heart on the one hand, and a beast's heart on the other, that is, human sympathies and those of the brutes, cannot be predicated of a tree, and therefore this part of the prophecy is *not symbolical, but verbal.** The

* The transition from the symbolical to the verbal, as we stated in the first chapter, begins in the latter part of verse 15th—"and let his portion be with the beasts of the earth.

16. "Let his heart be changed from man's," &c.

language here used is not applicable to the tree which was the symbol, but only to Nebuchadnezzar, who was the person symbolized; and it is over *him*, and not over the tree, that the *seven times* are said to pass, and hence they are to be interpreted accordingly. The prediction, therefore, of the *seven times*, in Dan. iv. 16, was part of *a verbal prophecy* which foreshowed that Nebuchadnezzar should be deprived of his reason, and be degraded for seven years from the dignity and glory of a man, to the level of a brute. How, then, does this chronological period *in a verbal* prophecy disprove the law under consideration, which has reference exclusively to *symbolical* prophecy?

So, also, the *seven times*, in the twenty-sixth chapter of Leviticus, are *not symbolical.* The Hebrew שֶׁבַע* in Lev. xxvi. 18, 21, 24, 28, is equivalent in that connexion to *sevenfold*, and denotes not the duration but the intensity of the judgments which the Lord would inflict upon the Israelites in case of their disobedience. The

* Forma שֶׁבַע etiam est adv. *septies.*—Lev. xxvi. 18, 21. Gesenius's Hebrew Lexicon, Leipsic ed. 1833, p. 979, column 2d.

In the passages in Leviticus xxvi., there is no word in the original to correspond with the English word "*times*," as there is in Dan. iv.

language of that chapter is not descriptive of any symbolization which had been perceptible either naturally, or in dreams, or in ecstatic vision. The prophecy is exclusively verbal, and therefore is not to be adduced either for or against the law in question.

If it be further objected that the three years during which Isaiah was to walk "naked and barefoot," represented a three years' captivity of the Egyptians and Ethiopians, Is. xx. 3, 4, we answer that the Hebrew* phrase translated *three years*, does not necessarily belong to the emblematical condition of the prophet, but may be rendered as referring to the captivity of which that condition was a symbol, and then the meaning of the original will be, as in Bp. Lowth's version, "a sign . . of three years."† So, also, the Vulgate—"trium annorum signum."‡ Bp. Lowth conjectures that the symbolical act of the prophet lasted only three *days*. If that was the fact, then this case, in respect to the point before us, resembles that of Ezekiel, who was directed

* See Alexander in loco, 8vo. edition, 1846, p. 372.

† Translation of Isaiah, with a preliminary dissertation and notes, by Robert Lowth, D.D., &c., Bishop of London, 8vo. London edition, 1825, pp. 113, 308, 309.

‡ Antwerp Polyglott in loco, p. 58.

to lie on his side "*each day for a year*," Ezek. iv. 6, and is precisely according to the law of symbols, *the three days representing three years.* No one can prove from the original Hebrew that the symbolical action of Isaiah continued longer than three days, and therefore this passage, Is. xx. 3, presents no valid objection to the law which we have endeavored to establish.

The evidence, therefore, already adduced in support of the law, remains unimpeached, and most clearly and conclusively demonstrates that, *in the circumstances stated in the law, days symbolize years.*

CHAPTER X.

BRIEF RECAPITULATION, in which it is shown that the symbols interpreted in the prophecies are interpreted by these laws —that interpretations of one or more of each class of symbols are given in the prophecies—and that these inspired interpretations are to be regarded as a revelation of the principle applicable to all the symbols, and the laws by which they are framed revealed laws.

WE have thus carefully examined the foregoing laws of symbolization, and have sustained them by the most abundant scriptural evidence; and from what has been already said it is manifest that THE SYMBOLS INTERPRETED IN THE PROPHECIES ARE INTERPRETED BY THESE LAWS.

This we have shown in the case of a large number of inspired interpretations, and not a single instance can be adduced from the *visions* of the Hebrew prophets, or from the cases where those prophets or other real men were employed *naturally* as representative agents, or from the *dreams* respecting the great image and the great tree, in which prophetic symbols are interpreted in the sacred volume on any other principle. The exception in regard to the dream of Pharaoh, king of Egypt, has been shown not to affect the general laws of symbolization. It is evident, therefore, that *the symbols interpreted in the prophecies are interpreted by these laws.*

Again:—INTERPRETATIONS OF ONE OR MORE OF EACH CLASS OF SYMBOLS ARE GIVEN IN THE PROPHECIES.

Among the symbols of each class of which, as we have shown in the previous discussions, there is an inspired interpretation, either directly or by implication, in the context, may be mentioned the following:—

God the Father, Rev. iv., v.; the Lamb, Rev. v., vi., xiv.; the Word, Rev. xix. 13, which are divine:—

Angels, devils, and men, Rev. xii. 7–12, &c., which are created intelligences:—

Beasts, such as a lion, a bear, a ram, and a goat, Dan. vii., viii., which are unintelligent or irrational creatures:—

A ten-horned wild beast, with iron teeth and nails, or claws of brass, a winged lion, a four-headed leopard, Dan. vii., which are monster animals:—

Waters, Rev. xvii. 1, 15, which are a symbol from the natural world:—

Candlesticks, Rev. i. 12, 20, and an image, Dan. ii., which are artificial objects :—

A *day* symbolizing a *year*, which is a shorter period representing an analogous longer period, Ezek. iv. 6, "I have appointed thee *each day for a year* :"—

The prophets Isaiah, Is. xx., and Ezekiel, Ezek. iv., which are examples where real men, as distinguished from those seen in vision, are by divine direction employed as symbols :—

The great image and the stone from the mountain, Dan. ii., and the fourth beast, Dan. vii., which are examples of symbolic agents and objects existing only in dream or vision.

Several of the above-mentioned symbols, as for instance, the waters and the candlesticks, are examples, also, of the proper in distinction from the monstrous.

The act of the fourth beast, Dan. vii., in trampling on other animals, and the effect produced upon the great image, Dan. ii., by the agency of the stone, are examples in which an act symbolizes an act, and an effect represents an effect; and the strength of the iron and the brittleness of the clay, and their incapability of thorough union, are examples in which qualities, conditions, and characteristic relations, have their corresponding counterparts.

So that it cannot be denied that inspired interpretations *of one or more of each class of symbols* are given in the prophecies.

THESE INSPIRED INTERPRETATIONS, THEREFORE, ARE TO BE REGARDED AS A REVELATION OF THE PRINCIPLE APPLICABLE TO ALL THE SYMBOLS, AND THE LAWS BY WHICH THEY ARE FRAMED, REVEALED LAWS.

If the uninterpreted symbols admit of any consistent exposition, it must be on the principle of analogy and resemblance as here stated; and the fact that such a multitude of expositions of the symbols used have been given in the sacred volume, according to this very principle of analogy and resemblance, and one or more of every class, should be regarded as conclusive evidence that these inspired interpretations are designed as the key to all symbols of a like character. History, also, in every instance accords with the prophecies as thus explained, so far as they have yet been fulfilled; and this corroborates the view which we have taken.

Now, when by a large induction of facts a law has been demonstrated, in regard to material phenomena, and no fact can be brought forward at variance with the law, it is considered as settled. For the same reason we claim that these laws of symbolization, deduced from the inspired interpretations, and in every instance perfectly accordant with such interpretations, are to be considered as of universal application.

CHAPTER XI.

Results of these laws.

I. These laws obviate difficulties and give consistency and certainty to interpretation—proof and illustration of this by various examples, and particularly by an exposition of the drying up of the symbolical Euphrates, Rev. xvi. 12.

II. These laws show that to spiritualize the symbolic prophecies is altogether wrong.

III. The slaughter of the two apocalyptic witnesses, Rev. xi., foreshows a real, literal slaughter of the faithful followers of Christ thus represented—a slaughter which is yet future.

IV. The antichristian powers are to be destroyed, not converted.

V. There will be, anterior to the millennium, a real and literal resurrection of departed saints.

VI. The second coming of Christ will be *before* the millennium.

VII. There will be men living in the natural body on the earth *after* Christ's second coming.

Having thus demonstrated from the inspired volume the correctness of our laws of symbolization, we shall next consider some of their most

IMPORTANT RESULTS.

I. In the first place, it is evident from what has been already said, that these laws "obviate difficulties, remove uncertainties, supply important defects, give consistency and certainty to interpretation, and lead to a clear and demonstrable explication of many symbols, of which no satisfactory solution is obtained by other systems of construction."*

The truth of this remark will readily be perceived in its application to the first four seals, which we explained on pp. 38–40; the two apocalyptic witnesses, pp. 52–58;† the binding of Satan, pp. 62–64; the first resurrection, pp. 64–76;‡ the seven heads and seven mountains, p. 88 (Note); the body of the beast, p. 89 (Note); the harlot sorceress who rides upon the beast, and sits at the many waters, pp. 89–91; and the chronological periods, pp. 98–106.

Commentators in general, in the exposition of

* Circular respecting the Premium Essays—see Preface.

† See also below, pp. 121–124.

‡ See also below, pp. 126–131.

these and many other symbols which we have examined, have proceeded on no uniform and consistent scheme of interpretation. Thus, for example, Mr. Habershon and many others have adopted the principle of *a day for a year*, in regard to prophetical periods, but they have applied it to cases where it is not admissible, as to the *seven times*, in the twenty-sixth chapter of Leviticus, and in the fourth of Daniel, which we have shown are not symbolical, the former denoting the intensity of the chastisements which the Lord was to inflict on the Jewish nation in case of their disobedience; and the latter, the seven years' insanity of the king of Babylon. Mr. Elliott, who is one of the most learned and interesting writers on the Apocalypse, interprets the first four seals on the principle that the symbol is of the *same* species, order, rank, or kind, with the thing symbolized; but, in his explanation of the dragon and wild beast, he tacitly assumes the opposite principle, that they are of a *different* species or order, but gives no rule or law by which the student, who wishes to ascertain the true meaning of the symbolical prophecies, can tell when he is to be governed by the former principle, and when by the latter. There is the same deficiency in many other expository works of great erudition and research; and the consequence has been, that most persons have well nigh given up all hope of obtaining any certain and satisfactory solution of a large part of the prophetic symbols. If it be alleged that our own expositions are liable to the same objection, we answer no; for we have clearly stated and abundantly proved the laws of symbolization which apply to all such cases, pp. 34–77 (chapters iv. and v.). Many writers, also, instead of uniformly regarding symbols as *representative agents*, *objects*, &c., by means of which God revealed future events, have often spoken of them as if they were mere *figures of speech.* They have also interpreted symbolic *agents* as denoting *abstract principles*, explaining, for instance, the three unclean spirits, Rev. xvi. 13, as denoting three *principles* or *systems*, which is directly contrary to the law that *living agents represent living agents*, and *not* acts or *effects*, *not principles* or *systems.* But there is perhaps no one symbol which interpreters have more generally misapprehended than "the great river Euphrates," Rev. xvi. 12. The exhibition of its true import, with the refutation of the prevailing false construction, will be sufficient for the further illustration of the topic before us.

"And the sixth angel poured out his vial upon the great river Euphrates, and the water thereof was dried up."—Rev. xvi. 12.

The river Euphrates flowed through ancient Babylon, which was situated by its "many waters," Jer. li. 13. That great city was the symbol, in the visions of the Apocalypse, of apostate and persecuting hierarchies within the ten kingdoms. But the *waters* are symbolical as well as the city; and in all cases where the interpretation is according to analogy, such a symbol, as we learn from Rev. xvii. 15, denotes a multitude of people. "The waters which thou sawest, where the harlot sitteth, are peoples, and multitudes, and nations, and tongues." The waters of the Euphrates, therefore, in their symbolical import, must represent that mighty stream of people of different nations and languages, which sustains to the mystical Babylon a relation analogous to that which the literal Euphrates did to the literal Babylon. That ancient city was the commercial emporium of the world, and, by means of that great river, received into its bosom the wealth of the nations. From its impregnable ramparts the inhabitants laughed at all the efforts of the invader; and it was not until the trenches had been dug, and the waters diverted, and the river reduced to a shallow morass, that the conquest of the city could be effected. In like manner, when the vast stream of peoples and nations, which has carried wealth into the mystical Babylon, is diverted from its former channel, and the symbolical river dried up, the "great city" must fall. Thus the mystical Euphrates, Rev. xvi. 12, in symbolizing a grand obstacle to the downfall of the mystical Babylon, analogous to the literal Euphrates in its relation to the literal Babylon, denotes the great mass of people who have brought wealth and power to the apostate hierarchies.

The common interpretation, however, has been that the Euphrates symbolizes the rulers of the Turkish Empire; and consequently the drying up of its waters, the drying up of their resources. But do the rulers of the Turkish empire support any hierarchies in Western and South-Western Europe, the regions of the ten kingdoms? None whatever. Hence they sustain no such relation to the mystical Babylon as the literal Euphrates did to the literal Babylon, and therefore cannot be the persons symbolized.

The interpretation was based upon Isaiah viii. 7, 8, where it is said—"Now, therefore, behold, the Lord bringeth up upon them *the waters of the river* strong and many, even the king of Assyria, and all his glory, and he shall come up over all his channels, and go over all his banks. And he shall pass through Judah," &c. The waters of the Euphrates, referred to in that passage, were supposed to symbolize the king of Assyria; and hence it was argued, that as, in ancient times, the waters of the river symbolized the Assyrian monarch who then reigned upon its banks, so, in modern times, they must symbolize those who now rule upon its banks, to wit, the Turkish dynasty. But in Isaiah viii. 7, the phrase "*waters of the river*," is not descriptive of a symbol. No such object was then presented to the eye of the prophet, either naturally or in vision, nor is there any evidence that in that prediction it is in any respect used symbolically. The prophecy is there given entirely through the medium of words, and not of symbols. The phrase quoted from Isaiah is simply a metaphor. The king of Assyria, with his invading armies, is figuratively denominated "*the waters of the river strong and many*," and is therefore said to "come up over all his channels, and go over all his banks." That ancient monarch is the subject of the elliptical affirmation, by which he is called the waters of the river, &c., and the figure consists in predicating something concerning him which in a certain relation he strongly resembled, but which, in the literal sense of the words, was incompatible with his nature, it being impossible that a civil ruler, a human being, should be literally an inanimate river overflowing its banks. Hence the mistake of Mede, Edward Irving, Cunninghame, Faber, Elliott, Bickersteth, and others, in the interpretation of the sixth vial, arose from confounding metaphors with symbols. It is the more important to notice that confusion, as it frequently occurs; so much so that learned writers even speak of the apocalyptic New Jerusalem as a metaphor! Whereas, instead of a metaphor, it is a *symbol*, and the language which describes it is for the most part literal, and tells exactly what St. John saw in the vision, namely, a beautiful and magnificent city adorned like a bride, and descending from heaven. That city, as we shall hereafter show, is the symbol of redeemed and glorified men.

The drying up of the mystic Euphrates is now going on, and shows us the precise spot which we occupy on the great chart of prophecy. But it is one of the singular anomalies in the history of Europe, that while a multitude of people are withdrawing their support from the papal hierarchies, especially in Germany and Italy, and in some parts of Ireland, and while the Pope is kept upon his throne by a foreign force against the wishes of the Italians, his influence as an ecclesiastico-political ruler, a horn of the beast, Dan. vii. 8, is so great as to convulse to its centre a powerful country like England, and cause an agitation of which we have seen as yet only the beginning.

II. In the next place, these laws show that to spiritualize the symbolic prophecies is altogether wrong. If, for example, as we have already proved, *living agents always denote living agents*, and not mere abstract principles or systems, acts or effects, or inanimate objects, then the living Redeemer, visibly descending from heaven, Rev. xix. 11–16, cannot denote Christianity; the three frogs from out of the mouth of the dragon, and from out of the mouth of the beast, and from out of the mouth of the false prophet, Rev. xvi. 13, 14, cannot symbolize lawlessness, despotism, and superstition; the "two witnesses" or "prophets," two living men prophesying twelve hundred and sixty days, and then slain and rising from the dead, Rev. xi. 3–12, cannot mean the Old and New Testaments.

III. In the third place, these laws demonstrate

that the slaughter of the two apocalyptic witnesses, Rev. xi., foreshows a real, literal slaughter of the faithful followers of Christ thus represented—a slaughter which is yet future.

The beast from the abyss symbolizes the civil rulers of the ten kingdoms; and the two witnesses represent certain churches and their line of ministers existing throughout the twelve hundred and sixty years, and bearing a faithful testimony for Christ during that whole period.

According to the laws of symbolization, living agents denote living agents, and acts foreshow acts. The act of the wild beast, therefore, in killing the witnesses, must symbolize a corresponding act on the part of those rulers towards these followers of Jesus. The slaughter of pious men by a ferocious beast, is well fitted to represent the murder of such men by sanguinary rulers, the witnesses here symbolizing those of their own order, kind, or species, agreeably to a law already established; but the mere act of silencing their testimony, which has been the common interpretation, does not by any means come up to the full significance of the symbol. Those who advocate such an exposition maintain that that part of the prophecy has been already fulfilled, which is contrary to historical fact. Whe ther we explain the prediction as referring to two churches and their ministers, or give it a wider application, the witnesses have never been silenced. The mere fact, upon which so much stress is laid by Mr. Elliott, that those whom he considers the witnesses did not appear when summoned before a Papal Council, and the orator of the Pope exclaimed in triumph on the 5th of May, 1514—*jam nemo reclamat, nullus obsistit*—"*now no one gainsays, no one opposes*," is no evidence that they were either dead or had ceased to testify for Jesus. The council itself, as Elliott has shown, was an antichristian abomination, and the witnesses for Christ were under no obligation either to respect or acknowledge its authority. Such witnesses have never yet become wholly extinct within the territory of the old Western Roman Empire, and, ever since Christianity was planted there by the apostles, they have always testified, and do still testify for the truth as it is in Jesus. Hence, as those of Christ's faithful followers who are represented by the two apocalyptic witnesses, have never been silenced, such an interpretation is inadmissible. It is inadmissible for two reasons: first, because it is contrary to analogy; and next, because it is contrary to historical fact. Though from the necessity of the case, the symbol may sometimes fall short, in some respects, of the thing symbolized, yet as the latter never falls short of the former, there must thus far be a correspondence between them; and therefore the literal, corporeal death of these two witnesses* must foreshow the corresponding death of those whom they represent. Nothing short of that can come up to the significance of the symbol. If, as it has been well remarked, the symbolic act on the part of the wild beast had been a mere obstructing of the vocal organs of the two witnesses, then the silencing of their testimony might have been the thing foreshown. But the symbolic slaughter of the witnesses was something very far beyond a mere obstructing of the powers of speech, and has a corresponding analogy in nothing short of the literal and corporeal slaughter of those faithful followers of Jesus whom the witnesses represent; and therefore that is the event which is thus foreshown.

Again, the slaughter here symbolized, Rev. xi., is yet future.

* It is not formally mentioned that the symbolic witnesses were seen by the prophet in a state of corporeal death, but it is implied in the symbolic representation, described verses 11, 12, Rev. xi., in which those witnesses were seen rising from death, and ascending to heaven.

This is evident from two considerations: first, because there has never yet been, *on a scale sufficiently comprehensive to correspond with that which is here foreshown by the symbols*, a slaughter of Christ's faithful followers by the rulers of the Western Empire, since the commencement of the twelve hundred and sixty years; and next, because the period during which those represented by the two witnesses were to continue their testimony, and then to be slain, Rev. xi. 2, 7, has not yet expired.

The two witnesses, as we have already seen, represent certain churches and their respective lines of pastors; and the wild beast denotes the persecuting civil rulers of the ten kingdoms; but when have these rulers ever yet slain all of those whom the two witnesses represent? Never.

Again, the commencement of the twelve hundred and sixty years cannot, with any probability, be dated earlier than the time when the Roman Catholic religion was established by law throughout the ten kingdoms; and as that appears to have been either almost at the end of the sixth century, or soon after the beginning of the seventh, the period has not yet expired. It follows, therefore, that the epoch for that slaughter of the witnesses which is foreshown in the eleventh chapter of the Apocalypse, though not far distant, is still future.

IV. In the fourth place, it is evident from these laws that the antichristian powers are to be destroyed, not converted.

According to the laws of symbolization there is a resemblance or analogy between the symbol and the thing symbolized. Now, in the symbolic representation recorded Rev. xix. 20, the beloved disciple saw the beast and the false prophet "cast alive into a lake of fire burning with brimstone." But there is no analogy or resemblance between such an event and the conversion of those here symbolized. It can foreshow nothing short of a terrible and remediless destruction.

The same thing is evident from the symbolization in Dan. ii. 34, where it is said that the stone from the mountain smote the great image upon the feet, and crushed it in pieces. The destruction of the great image by the stone clearly foreshows that the rulers symbolized by the image will meet with a corresponding destruction from those symbolized by the stone. As the fourth kingdom, Dan. ii. 40, was with its iron strength to "*break in pieces*" its adversaries, so the kingdom which God is to establish in the latter days is to "*break in pieces* and consume all these kingdoms," and to "stand for ever," Dan. ii. 44. The same crushing violence is predicted, according to the inspired interpretation of the symbols, in the one case as in the other.

So, also, in Dan. vii. 11, the utter destruction of the wild beast, and the giving of his body to the burning flame, can foreshow nothing short of an utter destruction of those whom the wild beast symbolized. The antichristian powers, therefore, are to be destroyed, not converted.

It will not do to say that all that is foreshown by the destruction of the beast and the false prophet and their armies, is the destruction of their systems of error, for we have already demonstrated that living agents symbolize *living agents*, and *not acts or effects, not principles or systems.* See chapters I. and III.

V. In the fifth place, the laws of symbolization demonstrate that anterior to the age of blessedness, purity, and peace, commonly called the millennium, there will be a real and literal resurrection of departed saints.

This is evident from the symbolization in Rev. xx. 4. We have already proved that a real and literal resurrection is there foreshown.* Some

* See the two resurrections discussed under the third law of prophetic symbols, pp. 64–75.

of the commentators object to such an interpretation of verses 4–6, on the ground that the Apocalypse is a book of symbols, and that therefore it is absurd to suppose that a literal resurrection is here indicated; but these very same commentators, with strange inconsistency, interpret verse twelfth, a little further on in the chapter, as denoting precisely that kind of resurrection! If the symbolic character of the book is a valid objection to the interpretation which maintains that a literal resurrection is foreshown in verse fourth, it is equally so to the interpretation which maintains that a literal resurrection is foreshown in verse twelfth. But the laws of symbolization demonstrate, as we have already proved, that both the one and the other are literal resurrections, living agents representing living agents, acts denoting acts, and effects, effects; the symbolic pre-millennial resurrection of the saints, as seen in the vision, Rev. xx. 4, foreshowing a corresponding pre-millennial resurrection of the saints who are to be raised at Christ's coming; and the symbolic post-millennial resurrection of the wicked, as seen in the vision, Rev. xx. 12, 13, foreshowing a corresponding real resurrection of that class at that epoch. The "*blessed and holy*" have part in "*the first resurrection*,"

Rev. xx. 6; "*the rest of the dead,*" Rev. xx. 5 have part in the second resurrection.

Again, it is expressly stated that the blessed and holy who have part in the first resurrection, reign with Christ during "the thousand years;" and therefore their resurrection is anterior to that period. There is no reason to believe that at that epoch any of the holy dead will be left unglorified. The symbolization represents a collection of persons sitting on thrones, among whom two classes are specified, first the martyrs, and next those who had not worshipped the beast, neither his image, neither had received his mark upon their foreheads or in their hands. There were many of this class who had not been slain. There were also multitudes of the righteous who lived before the reign of the beast; and who, having been faithful servants of the Lord, will then be openly rewarded. These, doubtless, are included in the number of regal saints whom St. John saw sitting upon thrones. The crown, we are expressly told by St. Paul, will be given by the Lord, the righteous Judge, to all them that love his appearing, 2 Tim. iv. 8.

The doctrine of the first resurrection, which in Rev. xx. 4, is taught through the medium of symbols, is implied in many passages which describe no symbolic representation whatever, and which must, therefore, be interpreted by the laws of language.

Take one from the Old Testament and one from the New to corroborate our conclusion.

The doctrine under consideration is implied in Zech. xiv. 5. "THE LORD my God SHALL COME, AND ALL THE SAINTS WITH THEE." What this prediction means is clear from the similar language used by St. Paul in speaking of the second coming of Christ, and the resurrection of the saints —"To the end he may stablish your hearts unblameable in holiness before God, even our Father, at THE COMING OF OUR LORD Jesus Christ WITH ALL HIS SAINTS," 1 Thess. iii. 13. The identity of language in the two cases shows that the event spoken of in Zechariah is the second coming of our Lord Jesus Christ, God manifest in the flesh, attended by his risen and glorified saints; and the context in Zechariah, that it is pre-millennial, for it precedes the destruction of the antichristian confederacy against Jerusalem, after which, as we learn from the concluding part of that chapter, the millennium is ushered in, and holiness generally prevails.

This doctrine is implied, also, in Phil. iii. 11, where St. Paul represents himself as ready to make any sacrifice, if he could only "attain unto the resurrection from amongst the dead." The common reading of the Greek is τὴν ἐξανάστασιν τῶν νεκρῶν, where the preposition ἐκ (which before a vowel becomes ἐξ), in composition with the word ἀνάστασιν, makes the phrase equivalent to ἀνάστασιν ἐκ τῶν νεκρῶν, and the literal translation is that which we have given above. The reading in the critical edition of the Greek Testament by Dr. M. A. Scholz, of Leipsic, is still stronger, containing a repetition both of the article τὴν and the preposition ἐκ—εἰς τὴν ἐξανάστασιν τὴν ἐκ νεκρῶν—*unto the resurrection which is from out of dead ones.* The resurrection here spoken of by the apostle is thus an eclectic resurrection, the righteous being taken from out of the collective mass of the dead, and the wicked left behind. If there be no first resurrection, as distinguished from a second, if it be the purpose of God that both the righteous and the wicked shall rise simultaneously, why should St. Paul express it as the object of his highest hopes to attain unto the resurrection? It was precisely for the very reason that there *is* such a distinction as we have noticed, and that *the first resurrection*, at the appearing of Christ, when the regal saints are to sit with the Son of man upon the throne of his glory, Rev. iii. 21, Matt. xxv. 31, is *the peculiar privilege of the righteous*, that the apostle was pressing forward with untiring ardor, through evil and through good report, in order to obtain it.

VI. In the sixth place, it is evident from these laws that the second coming of Christ will be *before* the millennium.

The symbolization in Rev. xix., where the glorified Redeemer appears for the destruction of the antichristian rulers and their organized confederacy, clearly foreshows a personal and visible manifestation. His visible descent from heaven is evidently symbolical of his visible descent to the earth; and his being followed by the risen and glorified saints on this work of retribution, shows that at the epoch denoted by the vision, their resurrection will have taken place. But the destruction of the antichristian confederacy is before the general prevalence of holiness and peace, or in other words, before the age of millennial blessedness. The coming of Christ, therefore, which precedes that destruction must also be pre-millennial.

It is only by false principles of interpretation that our opponents can avoid this conclusion. If, instead of spiritualizing the symbolic prophecies, they admitted and followed the laws of symbolization which have been demonstrated in this Essay, they would grant that the second coming of Christ is before the millennium.

Again, it is evident from the symbolization in Rev. xx. 4, as we have already proved, that the resurrection of the saints is pre-millennial; but the Scriptures teach us that the second coming of Christ is at the same epoch—"Christ the first fruits; afterward they that are Christ's AT HIS COMING," 1 Cor. xv. 23—and therefore that coming is pre-millennial.

The result at which we have thus arrived from the laws of symbolization, is corroborated by a multitude of unsymbolical prophecies. Take, for example, the verbal prediction in 2 Thess. ii. 8—"Then shall that wicked (or Lawless One, ὁ ἄνομος) be revealed whom the Lord shall consume with the spirit of his mouth, and destroy with the brightness of his coming." The whole context shows that the coming of which Paul speaks in that passage, is the second personal and visible appearing of the Lord Jesus Christ, which the Thessalonians thought was instantly impending, and in view of which they had become agitated and alarmed. But as the destruction of Antichrist is admitted to be pre-millennial, the personal and visible coming of Christ, to effect that destruction, must be pre-millennial also.

VII. In the seventh place, these laws clearly show that there will be men living in the "natural body" upon the earth *after* the second coming of Christ.

The glorified church is symbolized in the Apocalypse by the holy city, New Jerusalem, for that city, as we learn from Rev. xxi. 9, 10, represents the same class of persons as are denoted by the Bride, the Lamb's wife; and in another vision, Rev. xix. 8, the Bride is exhibited as "arrayed in fine linen, clean and white," a symbolic badge which is explained as indicating "the righteousness of the saints," τῶν ἁγίων, and which identifies also the warrior horsemen who follow the Lord Jesus Christ in his descent from heaven, Rev. xix. 11–21, on the work of retribution.

Now, as the holy city New Jerusalem symbolizes the glorified church, the nations who walk in the light of that city, Rev. xxi. 24, and are thus distinguished from the city itself, must represent nations composed of living men in the "natural body," *unglorified* inhabitants of the earth at that epoch, who are to be guided by the teachings which Christ communicates to his regal, *glorified* saints, and through them, as his as sociate "*kings and priests*," βασιλεῖς καὶ ἱερεῖς, Rev. v. 10, xx. 6, to the subjects of their concurrent jurisdiction. And all this is clearly *after* the second coming of Christ, for it is not until that coming that the descent of those who are symbolized by the New Jerusalem is to take place.

Now it is clear that the *regal saints* who are associated in the dominion with Christ, are glorified men in the "spiritual body," and not unglorified men in the "natural body;" for neither in the symbolical nor the verbal prophecies are the men in the natural body ever exhibited as, in that state, reigning with Christ over the kings and nations of the earth. That is the prerogative of those who are symbolized by the New Jerusalem, in whose light walk "the nations of the saved," and within whose walls "the kings of the earth do bring their glory and honor," Rev. xxi. 24. It is either by their resurrection from the dead, or by their living transfiguration into glory from the "natural" to the "spiritual," that men are exalted to the condition of those who are symbolized by that holy city.

Among the *regal saints* must be classed the blessed and holy that had part in the first resurrection, and were seen in the vision, Rev. xx. 4, *sitting upon thrones*, and who lived and reigned with Christ during the thousand years. The men seen in that vision, as we have already shown, symbolize the real men who are to be raised in spiritual bodies at Christ's second coming, and exalted to thrones in the regeneration of glory.

In the number of the regal saints must also be ranked, after their transfiguration, those believers who at the epoch of Christ's advent to judgment (when he is descending to the earth to take possession of his throne, compare Zech. xiv. 4), are to be "changed in a moment, in the twinkling of an eye at the last trump," 1 Cor. xv. 51, 52, and caught up alive together with the risen saints to meet the Lord in the air, and to be, in consequence of this translation to glory, for ever with the Lord. In the language of the apostle—"The Lord himself shall descend from heaven with a shout, with the voice of the archangel, and with the trump of God; and the dead in Christ shall rise first. Then we which are alive and remain shall be *caught up together with them* in the clouds, to meet the Lord in the air; and so shall we ever be with the Lord," 1 Thess. iv. 16, 17. That these translated believers are to be associated in the kingly sway with Christ and the risen saints, may be inferred from the promise which is made to every victorious be liever of sitting with Christ upon his throne, Rev. iii. 21; the promise that those who suffer with him shall also reign with him, 2 Tim. ii. 12; and the express statement already cited from 2 Tim. iv. 8, that the crown is for all that shall have loved the appearing of Jesus.

Again, the destruction, which in the scenic representation, Rev. xix. 11–21,* is exhibited as being accomplished by *Christ* and the warrior horsemen or *glorified saints* (compare Psalm cxlix. 9—"to execute upon them the judgment written—this honor have all his saints"), is evidently the same as that which is foreshown by the crushing of the great image by *the stone*, Dan. ii. 34, 35. Hence *the destroying agents*, though represented in the two visions by different symbols, must be the same; and therefore,

* The False Prophet, Rev. xix., represents the same line of ecclesiastico-political chiefs that are symbolized, Dan. vii., by the little horn of the Fourth Beast. But that Fourth Beast symbolizes the same succession of rulers as are represented, Dan. ii., by the legs, feet, and toes of the great image. The rest of the Fourth Beast, Dan. vii., exclusive of the little horn, corresponds with the ten-horned beast of the Apocalypse. In our article in the Theological and Literary Journal for July, 1851, pp. 116–133, we have shown by a multitude of distinguishing characteristics that the Papal Dynasty is the one symbolized by that little horn.

the kings symbolized by the stone, and whose dominion was to extend over all the earth, Dan. ii. 35, 44, *are Christ and the glorified saints.*

Again, it is expressly revealed in Dan. vii. 27, compared with verse 14, that the regal saints (who, we have shown, are the glorified church) are, with Christ as their head, to exercise a dominion over "all *peoples* (Chaldee, עממיא, in the plural), nations, and languages," verse 14, "*under the whole heaven*," verse 27, that is, "*over all the earth*," Zech. xiv. 9, there being thus a manifest distinction between *the rulers of the kingdom and those who are its subjects.* But the latter class, the subjects of the kingdom, those who are described by the words, "*all peoples, nations, and languages*," are evidently men in the "natural body," for such is undeniably the import of that phraseology. The same identical words occur in Dan. vi. 25 (in the Chaldee, vi. 26), where they indisputably mean *the living population of the globe, men in the natural body*, speaking different languages, and inhabiting the earth; for such were the men to whom Darius wrote. The passage is as follows, and settles the import of the phrase under consideration: "*Then* king Darius wrote unto *all peoples, nations, and languages*, that dwell in all the earth." The same phraseology occurs with the same import in Nebuchadnezzar's decree, Dan. iv. 1 (in the Chaldee, iii. 31)—"Nebuchadnezzar the king unto *all peoples, nations, and languages*, that dwell in all the earth." There can be no question, therefore, that the subjects here spoken of, and over whom Christ and the saints of the Most High are to reign, Dan. vii. 14, 18, 27, are men in the natural body, and that they dwell on the earth. It is just as clear, also, that this is after the coming of the Lord, for the saints are not raised and glorified until that coming, and therefore cannot take possession of their kingdom till that epoch.

Again, the symbolic coming of the Messiah with the clouds of heaven, Dan. vii. 13, as seen in the vision, foreshows his real, visible coming in the great day; and his symbolic investiture with the dominion over all the nations, the corresponding real investiture with such a dominion at the epoch denoted. The dominion, therefore, exhibited in that vision, is a dominion which is to be manifested after Christ's second coming; and as it is over men in the natural body, and living on the earth, it follows that there will be such men on the earth after that event; and as the kingdom is to endure *for ever*, and the earth to be the scene of its manifestation, that there are always to be in this "everlasting kingdom" of "all peoples, nations, and languages," Dan. vii. 14, 27, unglorified subjects in the "natural body," as well as glorified rulers in the "spiritual body."

Let this mass of evidence be impartially weighed, and the conclusion is irresistible that there will be men living in the "natural body" upon the earth *after* the second coming of Christ.

CHAPTER XII.

ANSWER TO OBJECTIONS AGAINST THE SEVENTH RESULT.

1. Objection from what is said in 2 Pet. iii., respecting the perishing of the earth by fire.

2. Objection from the parable of the sheep and the goats, Matt. xxv. 31–46. The verbal prophecies confirm the view taken in the preceding chapter.

3. Objection from Christ's declaration, "my kingdom is not of this world," John xviii. 36.

4. Objection from Christ's delivering up the kingdom, 1 Cor. xv. 24–28.

5. Objection from the post-millennial revolt, Rev. xx. 7–9.

6. Objection from the limited extent of the earth, and the insufficiency of its means of nutrition. Moral impressiveness of the view here presented.

If it be asked how can there be men on the earth after Christ's second coming, when it is said in the Scripture that the earth is to perish by fire? we answer, it is said also in the Scripture, and in the same connexion, that the earth once perished by water, 2 Pet. iii. 6. If in perishing by water the earth was not annihilated, it is just as possible that in perishing by fire the earth may not be annihilated. As the world that now is, emerged at the command of the Lord from the flood of waters, so the world to come, at the command of that very Lord, who is "the same yesterday, to-day, and for ever," may emerge in new beauty and glory from the flood of fire; and as by the providence of God a seed was left to replenish the earth after its baptism by water, so also by the providence of that same God, "who worketh all things" according to "the counsel of his own will," a seed may be left to replenish the earth after its baptism by fire.

If it be asked how the preservation of a remnant of men in the natural body, after Christ's second coming, is compatible with the parable of the sheep and the goats, in the twenty-fifth chapter of Matthew, seeing that that parable includes all the individuals of the then living population of the globe? we answer, that although it is probable that the phrase πάντα τὰ ἔθνη, "*all the nations*," here denotes, exclusively, nations of living men in the natural body, inasmuch as that is its general, and perhaps uniform import in the Scriptures, and as there is no intimation in the parable that those who are here spoken of are persons raised from death, still, whatever in that respect be the true meaning of the phrase in question, there is decisive evidence in the parable itself, that that phrase does *not* include, in the most unrestricted sense, *all the individuals* of all the nations, and therefore presents no evidence against the fact that there may, nevertheless, be *other persons in the natural body* besides those here called the sheep and the goats. When nations are spoken of in their collective capacity, either as exerting an agency themselves, or as the subject of an agency exerted by others, the meaning commonly is, either that the official delegates and representatives of those nations, or else *a multitude of individuals* from among those nations, exert or are the subjects of such agency. Thus, when it is said in Zech. xiv. 2, "I will gather *all nations* against Jerusalem to battle," no one supposes that the phrase "*all nations*" means, in the most absolute and unlimited sense, *every man, woman, and child*, but *a multitude of people from all those nations;* in that case, all the nations as represented by their armies. When Christ says to the disciples, Matt. xxiv. 9, "and ye shall be hated by all the nations," ὑπὸ πάντων τῶν ἐθνῶν, it cannot mean *all the individuals* of all the nations, for, to say nothing of the thousands of infants who cannot be supposed to have had these feelings of hostility, the disciples had many converts among the nations, and those converts must be exceptions. The phrase, therefore, in that passage, also denotes *a multitude of people among all those nations;* and such is its import in the thirty-second verse of the twenty-fifth chapter of Matthew, where it is said, "and before him shall be gathered all *the nations,*" πάντα τὰ ἔθνη—that is, those who might be considered as in some sense representing all the nations.

That this language does *not* include, in the most unrestricted sense, *all the individuals* of the earth's population, is evident from the fact that there are very many persons who, either from extreme youth, or from other causes, have not access to the sick, and the naked, and the hungry, and the imprisoned, and consequently have not performed the deeds done in behalf of Christ's suffering disciples, by those called "*the sheep,*" or been guilty of the cold neglect which is charged upon "*the goats.*" It follows, therefore, that those who are designated as "the sheep and the goats," will *by no means* include *all the individuals* of the nations living upon the earth at the epoch of Christ's second coming; and hence the parable furnishes no evidence against the fact in question.

That there will be a remnant of men in the natural body on the earth after Christ's second coming, is not only taught in symbolic prophecy, as we have shown in the preceding chapter, but is expressly stated in the verbal prophecies; for example, in Isaiah lxvi. 15, 16, 18, 19, 20, and Zechariah xiv. 1–5, 16–18, where, *after the coming of the Lord with all his saints*, Zech. xiv. 5, and his pleading "by fire and by his sword . . with all flesh," Isaiah lxvi. 16, compare 2 Thess. i. 7, 8, a remnant is still spoken of in such language as this: "And it shall come to pass that *every one that is left of all the nations* which came against Jerusalem, shall even go up from year to year to worship the King, the Lord of hosts," &c., Zech. xiv. 16; and, "I will gather all nations and tongues, and they shall come and see my glory. And I will set a sign among them, and I will send *those that escape of them* unto the nations, to Tarshish, Pul, and Lud, that draw the bow, to Tubal, and Javan, to the isles afar off, that have not heard my fame, neither have seen my glory; and they shall declare my glory among the Gentiles. And they shall bring all your brethren for an offering unto the Lord out of all nations, upon horses and in chariots, and in litters, and upon swift beasts, to my holy mountain Jerusalem, saith the Lord," Is. lxvi. 18, 19, 20. In the parallel passage in Zech. xiv. 16–18, the nations or "*families of the earth*" are threatened with the deprivation of rain in case of their neglect to worship the King, the Lord of Hosts, in the manner prescribed; and the nation or "family of Egypt . . . . that have no rain," is threatened, in case of similar neglect, with "the plague." Who can doubt that the planet on which we dwell, the material globe, is the place to be inhabited by the nation or family of Egypt, and the other families of the earth referred to in these passages, and that the nations spoken of are nations of living men in the natural body, at the epoch to which these prophecies refer? The destruction from which they are to escape, as is evident from the context, is the one which is to occur at the coming of the Lord with all his saints, Zech. xiv. 1–5, and therefore this remnant is still to live *after* that coming. That there is to be such a remnant on the earth in its renewed state, is still further evident from the description of the "*new earth*," in Isaiah lxv. 17–25, *where it is expressly said*, in speaking of *men living in the natural body* at that epoch, *that such men are to build, and plant, and have offspring*—"they shall *build* houses and inhabit them; and they shall *plant* vineyards and eat the fruit of them . . . they shall not labor in vain, nor bring forth for trouble; for they are the seed of the blessed of the Lord, and their *offspring* with them," verses 21, 23, with which compare verse 17. Whatever difficulty, therefore, there may be in reconciling such statements of the inspired word with other revealed truths, it is clear from these express declarations that there will be at that epoch on the "*new earth*," Isaiah lxv. 17, compare 2 Peter iii. 13, a seed of men in the natural life—men who, as we have already shown, are to be enlightened by instruction from the glorified saints—in the language of the Apocalypse, "*nations*" who are to "*walk in the light*" *of the Holy City, New Jerusalem*, which is the symbol of those saints.

If it be asked, again, how are these views consistênt with Christ's declaration, John xviii. 36, "my kingdom is not of this world?" we answer, the unworldly nature and origin of Christ's kingdom are in no respect incompatible with the existence of men in the natural body on the earth after his second coming. If he can, *at this present moment*, administer an unworldly kingdom over men in the natural body—and that he does, our opponents believe as well as we—then most assuredly he can continue to administer an unworldly kingdom over such men after his second coming. If the mere fact, that the subjects of Christ's kingdom are men in the natural body, would make it worldly *then*, that fact would make it worldly *now*. But as it confessedly does not have that influence *now*, neither will it *then*. How, therefore, does the declaration, "my kingdom is not of this world," prove that there will not be men in the natural body on the earth after Christ's second coming?

Again, according to the views of our opponents themselves, the subjects of Christ's *millennial* sway will be men in the natural body on the earth: but if that fact make the kingdom a worldly one, then, *on their own theory*, Christ's administration during the thousand years would be a worldly administration; and if in this consists the point of the objection, it is one which refutes itself.

If it be said by our opponents, that they be

lieve that during the millennium the king will be invisible, and that his presence and reign, instead of personal, will be exclusively spiritual, while on the other hand we maintain that the king will be visible, and his presence and reign personal as well as spiritual; we answer, how does the fact of visibility necessarily make the kingdom a worldly one? That fact will not alter the pure and heavenly principles of Christ's government, or nullify their celestial origin. If his high and holy administration is free from carnality, while he conceals himself from our view, where is the impossibility of its being wholly free from it after he appears in his glory?

If it be said that we maintain that, after Christ's second coming, his glorified saints are to be associated with him in the kingly sway over all peoples, nations, and languages, under the whole heaven? we answer, very true; but that fact will not make the kingdom a worldly one. The principles of administration, instead of being imperfect or unjust, like those which often prevail in this world, will evince, by their unrivalled excellence, their heavenly origin. How, then, do the views which we have advocated conflict with Christ's declaration, "my kingdom is not of this world?" The kingdom which he now administers does not partake of the corrupt spirit of the world, its principles did not originate in the world, and therefore it is certainly not a *worldly* kingdom; nor will its visible manifestation, after his second coming, entail upon it that character. It is now a kingdom *over* this world, and its subjects are *in* this world, and what is more, *Christ the king was personally and visibly present* in his humanity, when he said, "my kingdom is not of this world," and therefore that declaration does not necessarily imply either that the king will always be personally absent from this province of his dominions, or that he will have no subjects in the natural body on the earth after his second coming. But if Christ's kingdom is not now a *worldly* kingdom in any objectionable import of the term *worldly*, it is evident from what has been said that in no such import will it be a *worldly* kingdom "when he shall come to be glorified in his saints, and to be admired in all them that believe." It will not be worldly either in its nature or its origin, for it is "*not from hence.*" Its chief rulers will not be the dwellers in the flesh, they will be Christ and the glorified saints; and the principles of their administration, instead of being corrupt and selfish, like those which are now dominant in the world, will be pure and heavenly.

But the futility of this objection will be still more apparent, when we turn to the context of the passage which is supposed to occasion the difficulty.

Christ had been accused before Pontius Pilate of sedition, of plotting the overthrow of Cæsar's government, in order to make himself a king in his stead. Pilate asked him, "What hast thou done?" Jesus answered, "My kingdom is not of this world; if my kingdom were of this world, then would my servants fight, that I should not be delivered to the Jews; but now is my kingdom not from hence," John xviii. 35, 36. The phrase translated, "*not of this world*"—οὐκ . . . ἐκ τõυ κόσμου τούτου—is, literally, "not *from* this world." The passage may be illustrated by the question which the Saviour put to the Jews, Matt. xxi. 25, "The baptism of John, whence was it? ἐξ *from* heaven, or ἐξ *from* men?" The Greek preposition in John xviii. 36, is ἐκ, and in Matt. xxi. 25, the same preposition changed into ἐξ before a vowel, and it means, *from, out of.* Baptism was indeed *a sacred rite of divine origin;* it was "*from heaven,*" but nevertheless, it was administered by John *personally and visibly* on earth. So in regard to the kingdom of Christ. *Its origin* is from the same source with the baptism of John, "*not from this world*," but from heaven, and after the second coming of Christ it is to be administered by the Saviour and his glorified saints *personally and visibly on the earth.* As Jesus was accused of sedition, of exciting the people against the existing government, it was enough for him to say in answer to the question, "What hast thou done?" I have done nothing to justify the charge; I have not stirred up the people against Cæsar; for my kingdom is not of this world; it is not of earthly but of heavenly origin; it is not to be established by the might of armies in the flesh, or upheld by human power; if it were, then would my servants fight that I should not be delivered to the Jews. But now is my kingdom not from hence. Such appears to have been, substantially, the import of our Saviour's answer to the Roman governor. The reply was pertinent to the circumstances of the case, and seems to have been satisfactory to Pilate.

There is a very important sense, therefore, in which Christ's kingdom is "*not of this world*," but that fact is in no respect at variance with our position, that there will be men in the natural body on the earth *after* his second coming.

If it be asked, again, how are these views compatible with what is said in the Bible respecting Christ's delivering up the kingdom, and consequently the termination of his office as Mediator, and the cessation of man's existence on the earth in the natural body? we answer, that although the Bible speaks of an event called the delivering up of the kingdom, it nowhere says that there is ever to be a termination of Christ's office as Mediator, or such a cessation of the human race. The passage referred to occasions no more difficulty for the millenarian than for the antimillenarian. That passage is as follows: "*Then cometh the end, when he shall have delivered up the kingdom to God, even the Father;* when he shall have put down all rule, and all authority, and power. For he must reign till he hath put all his enemies under his feet. The last enemy that shall be destroyed is death. For he hath put all things under his feet. But when he saith all things are put under him, it is manifest that he is excepted which did put all things under him. And when all things shall be subdued unto him, *then shall the Son also himself be subject unto him that put all things under him, that God may be all in all,*" 1 Cor. xv. 24–28. It is very true, that after the expiration of the millennium, and the final scenes of the judgment, death, the last enemy, shall be destroyed; but where is it said in this passage that there is to be a termination *of Christ's office as Mediator*, or that men are to cease to exist on the earth in the natural body after Christ's second coming? There is not a syllable to that effect. To say that it is implied either in the act of delivering up the kingdom, or in the phrase, "then cometh *the end*," is a mere gratuitous assumption. On the contrary, we are taught in the Scriptures that Christ is to be "*a priest for ever*, after the order of Melchizedec," Ps. cx. 4, Hebrews v. 6, vi. 20, vii. 21. As the existence of Christ in glorified humanity is eternal, it is therefore altogether possible that his *priesthood* should be *eternal*, and that, in the most absolute and unlimited sense, he should be "a high priest *for ever*," Heb. vi. 20. To say that the known nature of the subject limits the duration of that priesthood, and that therefore the words "*for ever*" must be taken in a qualified sense, is a mere begging of the question. The reason assigned by the apostle why his priesthood is unchangeable, is because his existence is *eternal*, and hence the fair inference from that fact is that *this priesthood*, which knows no change, is *eternal* also. After speaking of the mortality of the Jewish Levitical priests, the apostle adds, in respect to Christ: "But this man (Jesus), *because he continueth ever*, hath an unchangeable priesthood," Heb. vii. 24. If it be said that the word *ever*, as here used, is meant only to teach that as Christ continues to exist as long as the earth exists, therefore his priesthood can exist during that period, and that hence, as the existence of the earth is to cease, the priesthood must cease at the same time—we answer, that here again is a begging of one of the very points at issue, namely, that respecting the future eternity of this material globe. If it be said that the Scriptures speak of the burning up of the world, we answer, that we have already shown that it cannot be proved that the perishing by fire there spoken of, means *the annihilation* of the globe, for similar language is used by St. Peter respecting the former destruction by water. The destruction by fire is to result not in annihilation, but in renovation. The *earth* is to be *changed*, not struck out of existence. The old world, that is, "the world that then was" before the flood, perished by water, 2 Pet. iii. 6. "The heavens and the earth which are now," that is, the present earth with its surrounding atmosphere, is "reserved unto fire against the day of judgment and perdition of ungodly men," 2 Pet. iii. 7; but out of the wreck and ruin of that conflagration are to emerge, according to the promise, Isaiah lxv. 17–25, lxvi. 22, "new heavens and a new earth," that is, a new condition of the planet, with a new and purer atmosphere—"new heavens and a new earth, wherein dwelleth righteousness," 2 Pet. iii. 13. Where is it said in the Scriptures that the *new* earth, that is, this material globe in its renewed condition, is ever to be destroyed? Not a word to that effect. All that is said upon that subject would lead us to believe that the earth, after its baptism by fire, is to continue for ever. As the priesthood of Christ and the existence of the earth, as it respects the future, are to be eternal, so, also, according to the decisive evidence already presented, both from the symbolic and the verbal prophecies, there are to be men on the earth in the natural body after Christ's second coming, and as Christ ever liveth to make intercession for them, and present before his Father the infinite merits of his atoning sacrifice and death, the human race upon the earth, for aught that is said to the contrary, may exist for ever, and a blessed immortality, by virtue of the redemption which is in Christ Jesus, be given to them as the reward of their obedience. Those who are cast into the lake of fire are of course irretrievably lost, and remain an awful monument of God's inflexible abhorrence of sin; but as to those who, when death shall have been abolished, exist upon the earth in the natural body, after the last resurrection and final act of the judgment, the work of salvation may go on for ever.

We return to the question respecting Christ's delivering up the kingdom.

If the Father has intrusted to Christ a sceptre which the Saviour now wields over the universe—a sceptre which he is to continue to wield till the close of the millennium—and which, after the subjugation of all his foes, he is to return to him who gave it, that he may ever afterwards exercise his dominion in subordination to the Father, "that God may be all in all," 1 Cor. xv. 28, is it not just as possible for him in that new form of administration in which "the Son also himself shall be subject to him that put all things under him"—*is it not just as possible for him to exercise a dominion over men*, and that, too, over men *in the natural body*, provided that there are then such men—*is not this just as possible as it ever was?* Most assuredly. How, then, does the delivering up of the kingdom prove that the existence of the human race in the natural body is to cease? The fact under consideration affords not the slightest ground for that conclusion. Is it not just as possible, also, for Christ to deliver up the sceptre of millennial and pre-millennial rule, *when he has visibly appeared, and visibly reigned during the thousand years,*" *as it would be if he had, through that whole period, kept himself concealed from the view of his earthly subjects?* If the mere fact of visibility renders such a delivery impossible, if it cannot be done because there is *a public manifestation* of the splendors of his kingdom, then, our opponents themselves being judges, it cannot be done at all, for, according to their view, Christ is not only now visible in heaven, but is to continue thus visible there through the whole period of the millennium, and is to be visible somewhere, when "every eye shall see him," Rev. i. 7, in the scenes of the judgment. What difference, then, does it make in regard to the possibility of delivering up the kingdom, whether Christ's visible appearance take place before the millennium, or be delayed till after it is ended?

None whatever. This delivering up of the kingdom, therefore, is no argument either against Christ's pre-millennial advent and personal reign, or against the existence of the human race in the natural body on the earth after his second coming.

The order of events, as stated by the apostle, is this—"Christ the first fruits"—he passes over the interval between the first and second advents—"afterward, ἔπειτα, they that are Christ's at his coming"—he passes over again the interval between the first and second resurrections—"then (εἶτα,* afterward), the end"—the end of that chapter in Christ's high and holy administration—the end of his possession of that sceptre which he is to deliver up after the close of the millennium, and the subjugation of all his foes, that he himself also may be "subject unto him that put all things under him, that God may be all in all," 1 Cor. xv. 23, 24, 28. The apostle is speaking of the resurrection of the body, and events connected therewith, "As in Adam all die, even

* This is a particle denoting *succession*, not contemporaneousness, as is evident from Mark iv. 28, where we have this very particle εἶτα—"For the earth bringeth forth fruit of herself; first the blade, then (εἶτα, afterward) the ear, after that (εἶτα) the full corn in the ear."

so in Christ shall all be made alive. But every man in his own order (literally, *in his own band*); Christ the first fruits; afterward they that are Christ's at his coming. Then (or *afterward*) cometh *the end*," the end of that stage in his government, and the opening of a new scene in the history of the universe. If at that period death is to be abolished, and Christ to deliver up the sceptre which he has previously held, his enemies having been subjugated for ever, it is certainly a most marked epoch, and well may it be said, "*afterward* cometh *the end*," as there is an end of that *particular form* of rule which he will have thus far exercised. But where is there any intimation in this passage either that the work of the Mediator in sending his Holy Spirit to secure his subjects in obedience is to cease, or that men are no longer to exist in the natural body on the earth? There is none whatever. If the continued existence of the race in the natural body on the earth is elsewhere taught in God's sacred word, there is nothing to conflict with that fact in what is meant by Christ's delivering up the kingdom, and the consequent termination of that stage in his government, for it is clearly taught in the Scriptures, and admitted by all believers in the Bible, that in some form of administration, Christ will "reign for ever and ever," Rev. xi. 15; that "of his kingdom there shall be no end," Luke i. 33; and that "his dominion is an everlasting dominion, which shall not pass away," Dan. vii. 14. But that "dominion" is a dominion over "all peoples, nations, and languages," *ib.*, "under the whole heaven," Dan. vii. 26, "over all the earth," Zech. xiv. 9, phraseology which, as we have already proved, denotes men in the natural body on the earth, the subjects of that kingdom which is to be administered by Christ and the glorified saints. He is therefore to reign for ever, to be a priest for ever, a priest on his throne, and his glorified saints are to reign with him everlastingly. Is it not, then, perfectly compatible, that after what is called the delivering up of the kingdom, Christ, the Son of Man, with his beloved Bride, should be subordinate in office to the Eternal Father, and that at the same time the nations of living men should also be subordinate to them, and be holy and happy under their righteous and beneficent sway? Most assuredly. How, then, is there any incompatibility between this delivering up of the kingdom and the views which we have exhibited? Or how does that delivery prove either that Christ's office as Mediator is to cease, or that there will no longer be men in the natural body after Christ's advent to judgment?

The Scriptures have said but little respecting Christ's delivering up the kingdom to the Father, but aside from that, enough is revealed to prepare us for his coming. It is not necessary that we should, at present, know all the particulars of his millennial and post-millennial reign, or be able to explain the precise mode in which God will accomplish his high counsels of justice, mercy, and love. Our faith should rest in *the facts*, simply as they are revealed. It is enough, at present, for us to know that the sure word of prophecy informs us that Christ will, at his glorious appearing, raise from the dead the church of the first born, and translate those who are alive and remain, and love his appearing; that he will execute judgment on those who at his second coming are found in organized confederacy against him, and indeed upon all men in the natural life, except those whom, as the reward of their affectionate faith, he changes from mortal to immortal, and those whom in his infinite wisdom he saves from the general destruction, and leaves as a seed to replenish the earth, and to serve and obey him; that there will be an overwhelming and irremediable discomfiture of those of his unglorified subjects, who revolt from his sway at the expiration of the millennium, after Satan is loosed out of prison, and goes forth to deceive the nations; that he will raise the unholy dead to inflict upon them, in body and soul, in that complex nature in which they have sinned, the just recompense of their deeds; and that, having made this impressive demonstration of his supreme hatred of sin by the punishment of the wicked, he will abolish death, and reign for ever, in subordination to the Father, and in blissful association with his glorified church, "the Bride, the Lamb's wife," over a holy and happy creation.

If then it be asked again, how is the visible reign of Christ and the glorified saints over men in the natural body during the period represented by the thousand years, compatible with what is foreshown in Rev. xx., respecting the post-millennial revolt? we answer, that such a revolt will be just as possible, if Christ and the saints shall have been reigning in visible glory over such subjects, as if he alone, without these associate rulers, had been reigning over them in invisible glory. Probation is just as possible in the personal presence of Christ as in his absence.

The angels who, when on probation, rebelled against God, were doubtless in the presence of the Eternal Son, and if such probation was possible to angels, how does it appear that probation, when Christ is personally present on earth, is *per se* (*in itself*) impossible to men? If Satan, *with no one to seduce him*, could rebel *in heaven*, then most assuredly man, *when tempted by Satan*, can revolt on earth. If the personal presence of the Son of God did not prevent the fall of Satan, *an archangel of transcendent powers, when comparatively free from temptation*, how will that presence necessarily prevent the disobedience of unglorified men, *beings of very inferior powers*, and in the case before us, *under circumstances of very strong temptation?* Miraculous displays of divine power do not always prevent transgression. The children of Israel at the foot of Mount Sinai, after they had heard the voice of the living God, and seen the manifestations of his special presence, worshipped a golden calf; our first parents in Paradise, when perfectly holy, and enjoying the most intimate communion with their Creator, were seduced by the machinations of Satan; nay, in heaven itself, as we have just said, angels fell from their high estate, and revolted against the throne of God;

and in view of such facts, held by anti-millenarians themselves, where is the impossibility that Satan, when loosed out of prison, should succeed in deceiving a vast multitude among the nations, notwithstanding the visible displays of glory from Christ, their king? However quiet and peaceable they may have been under the dominion of Christ and the regal saints, while Satan was shut up in the abyss, and thus debarred from tempting them to evil, where is the impossibility of their revolting from that sway when Satan is loosed, and goes forth to deceive them? Such a revolt, therefore, is possible even among many who have lived during the millennium. It cannot, however, be proved that it extends to them. Whether it does, we know not. It may, perhaps, be confined to their descendants, to individuals living after the thousand years are ended. We are not told in the Scriptures how long is that "little season," Rev. xx. 3, in which Satan will once more be permitted to practise his wiles. It may be short, compared with the vast period denoted by the thousand years, and yet be long enough for him to exert his agency on a very large scale. New generations may grow up in that time, embracing many individuals who do not give their hearts to

Christ, individuals whom, in their comparative inexperience, it may be very easy for Satan to seduce in great numbers into open rebellion. In view, therefore, of all these facts, how does this post-millennial revolt conflict with the probation which Scripture elsewhere informs us will be given to those that are left from among the nations, and to their posterity?—a probation after the second coming of Christ, to men living in the natural body on the earth. There is no discrepancy whatever. But though successful in deceiving vast multitudes to their ruin, Satan suffers a final and hopeless defeat—his army is destroyed by the special interposition of God—and he himself consigned to the lake of fire, to be with those who are denoted by the beast and the false prophet, and to be "tormented day and night, for ever and ever," Rev. xx. 7–10.

The glorified saints have no part in that apostasy. Faithful to Christ as his Bride, united to him in bonds of the most ardent and unwavering love, secured in their holy and happy state by an everlasting covenant, they shall continue to reign upon Immanuel's throne for ever and ever, Rev. iii. 21, Dan. vii. 18, 27, Rev. xxii. 5.

The remnant of the human race in the natural body, those who have not been engaged in the post-millennial rebellion, confirmed in their allegiance by the influence of God's Holy Spirit, and by these awful judgments on the disobedient, will never revolt from the dominion of Christ and the saints. Death, the last enemy, will be destroyed; and, the curse having been removed, God will look forth upon his work and pronounce it, as it was when it first came from his hands, to be very good.

The post-millennial revolt, therefore, is no valid objection to the existence of men in the natural body after Christ's second coming. There are to be such men on the earth till the closing scenes of the judgment, and for aught that the Bible says to the contrary, there will be such men here through eternal ages. That, indeed, as we have already shown, is a legitimate inference from the fact that the kingdom of Christ and the glorified saints is an *everlasting* kingdom, and its subjects for ever, the men of all peoples, nations, and languages, under the whole heaven.

If, then, it be asked once more, how is that possible, in view of the limited extent of the earth, and the insufficiency of its means of nutrition, what can be done with so vast a population as there will necessarily be after death shall have been abolished, and men have continued to mul tiply through innumerable ages? where can they find space to dwell, or food to sustain them? we answer, there is no more difficulty in this case than there would have been if our first parents had not sinned, and death had never visited the race. The omnipotent Jehovah has resources inexhaustible, and we doubt not that *he* will be able to provide for the exigency. Successive generations, after being trained up for glory, may be changed from the natural to the spiritual body, and translated alive into a more exalted state as the reward of their obedience.

How vast, therefore, is the salvation which Christ is to accomplish! How inconceivably sublime are the results which shall send a thrill of ecstasy through all the obedient provinces of his exulting empire! What heaven can be more glorious or more desirable than a world rescued from the grasp of Satan; emancipated from death and sin; delivered from the curse; enlivened by the songs of countless myriads who will chant hallelujahs to God and the Lamb, when the tabernacle of God shall be with men, and he shall dwell among them; a world cheered by the personal as well as spiritual presence of Jesus; and governed by an administration perfect in wisdom and strength, holiness and love? Give me such a world, full of beings who are perfectly good and perfectly happy, in the presence of Christ, their Lord and Life, and I want no other heaven —give me, as a glorified saint, a share in that dominion which Christ has pledged to his beloved Bride, and let me have the promise and oath of God that this bliss shall know no end—that I with all his chosen shall be for ever holy and for ever happy—and I ask no more. I want no other paradise than such a world, with such inhabitants, and such enjoyments. I will rejoice with all my soul in the "new heavens and new earth wherein dwelleth righteousness."

If, as our opponents must admit, the scene in which, when raised from the grave and re-united to the soul, the bodies of the saints are to reside, is a material place, and if the most essential elements of its blessedness are the presence of Christ and holiness in the believer's heart, why then, so far as the mere locality is concerned, will not the new earth, surrounded by a pure and healthy atmosphere, and gladdened by the most tender and sacred associations, be just as good a heaven for the abode of the righteous, as some other place, in some distant quarter of the universe? Why will not this be as good a point as any other from which Jehovah may send forth glorified saints on missions of love to his dependent provinces?

Let the universe be ever so vast—let the telescope reveal system after system, throughout a crowded immensity—let suns, and planets, and stars, be indefinitely multiplied, still there must be some spot which shall be the metropolis of the universe; some favored place where the Deity specially manifests his presence; some palace-royal, where Jesus our king appears in his glory, and from which he sends forth ministering spirits to execute his behests; and why, then, may not the renewed earth be the pavilion where he shall hold his court? why may not this globe, on which he suffered and died—the scene of his humiliation—become the theatre of his triumph and tabernacle for ever?

CHAPTER XIII.

RESULTS—(Continued.)

VIII. The millennium is to continue three hundred and sixty thousand years.

IX. A series of the most stupendous events is not very far distant.

Having thus answered, and we hope satisfactorily, the main objections to the existence of men in the natural body on the earth after Christ's second coming, we shall notice, and that very briefly, but two other results of the laws of symbolization.

VIII. In the eighth place, these laws demonstrate that the millennium is to continue during three hundred and sixty thousand years.

We have already shown, that according to the mode of reckoning in Daniel and St. John, the equivalent expression for one thousand years, Rev. xx. 4, is three hundred and sixty thousand days, and that those days symbolize the same number of astronomical or solar years.

Take, therefore, the view to which we are led by the laws of symbolization, and what noble conceptions does this interpretation give us of the redemption which is in Christ Jesus! During these three hundred and sixty thousand years, under the beneficent sway of Christ and his glorified church, the boundless population of this rejoicing planet, undisturbed by the machinations of Satan, will walk in the paths of the Lord their Redeemer. What immense additions will be made to the happiness of the universe during the mighty roll of that vast succession of ages! While "the god of this world," 2 Cor. iv. 4, has rule, there are many who walk the broad road to destruction, and comparatively few that are saved; but ultimately, as God's plans become developed in the full manifestation of Messiah's reign, the number of the lost will bear but a small proportion to that countless throng who ascribe their eternal deliverance to God and the Lamb! Well may we exclaim—"Great and marvellous are thy works, Lord God Almighty; just and true are thy ways, thou king of saints!" Rev. xv. 3.

It is not to be inferred, however, that the reign of Christ and the saints is to cease at the expiration of the millennium. In the first part of the twentieth chapter of the Apocalypse, it is mentioned that Satan, according to the symbolization witnessed, was shut up in the bottomless pit. The symbolical period of his confinement is stated to be a thousand years; and then it is added, that during that period the saints lived again, and reigned with Christ. That, however, is only the first grand epoch of their associate sway. The sovereignty of Christ and his beloved Bride is to endure through eternal ages. Thus it is declared respecting the Messiah, in Dan. vii. 14, "his dominion is an *everlasting* dominion, which shall not pass away;" in Luke i. 33, "he shall reign over the house of Jacob *for ever;* and *of his kingdom there shall be no end;*" and in Rev. xi. 15, "he shall reign *for ever and ever.*" The same thing is said of the glorified saints in Rev. xxii. 5, "they shall reign *for ever and ever;*" in Dan. vii. 18, "the saints of the Most High shall take the kingdom, and possess the kingdom *for ever, even for ever and ever;*" and in verse 27, as Professor Stuart renders the Chaldee, "*their* kingdom shall be an *everlasting* kingdom, and all dominions shall serve and obey them."*

* The pronoun in the original is לְהּ, which means *it,* and refers for its antecedent to the word "*people,*" and therefore,

IX. In the ninth and last place, there is reason to believe that a series of the most stupen dous events is not very far distant.

The destruction of the antichristian rulers, civil and ecclesiastical, is to take place under the seventh vial, Rev. xvi. 17–21, xvii., xviii., xix. 2, 11–21, and, as we have already shown, p. 119, we are now living under the sixth. Those whc are symbolized by the apocalyptic witnesses testify to the truth as it is in Jesus, throughout the twelve hundred and sixty years; and according to the general opinion of the best interpreters of Scripture, more than twelve hundred years of that period* have already elapsed.

The slaughter of the witnesses, therefore, the gathering of all the chief rulers of the world, Rev. xvi. 14, to a general war, the second coming of Christ, the resurrection of the saints, the overthrow of those denoted by the Beast and False Prophet, the binding of Satan, and the age of millennial blessedness, are at hand.

according to the English idiom, must be rendered in the plural. "And the kingdom and dominion, and power of the kingdoms under the whole heaven, shall be given to *the people of the saints* of the Most High; *their* kingdom shall be an *everlasting* kingdom, and all dominions shall serve and obey *them*," Dan vii. 27.

* See above, p. 124.

CHAPTER XIV.

Conclusion.—Practical Reflections—the impending crisis—state of the visible church—duty of investigating all the Scriptures—testimony of the Holy Ghost to the utility of studying unfulfilled prophecy—grandeur of redemption—the ease with which the laws of symbolization may be mastered, and made the means of a large and useful knowledge of the prophecies—the claims of the subject upon the attention of Christians in general, and especially of ministers and teachers of the word—exhortation to trust and obey the Lord—origin, grandeur, and duration of the kingdom of Christ.

If these things are so, we are on the eve of a crisis unprecedented in the history of the world! But how utterly unprepared for these events is the great body of the visible church! The professed worshippers of the Lord are, for the most part, sunk in spiritual lethargy, wedded to sensual pomps and vanities, and unmindful of their high obligations as the betrothed of the Lord Jesus Christ.

When St. Paul wrote his second letter to the Thessalonians, they were apprehensive that the second coming of Christ in glorious majesty was immediately impending. The apostle told them that there must first be the rise of THE APOSTASY, 2 Thess. ii. 3, and the manifestation of THE MAN OF SIN. For more than twelve centuries there has been a most fearful apostasy from the truth as it is in Jesus; and the Papal "False Prophet," whom many believe to be the Man of Sin, has long exerted his blasphemous and persecuting agency. Nearly eighteen hundred years have passed away since Paul wrote to the Thessalonians, and therefore we are so much nearer to the second coming of Christ, by which the Man of Sin is to be destroyed, 2 Thess. ii. 8. But alas! how many there are who "know not, neither will they understand; they walk on in darkness," Ps. lxxxii. 5.

We rejoice, however, that the prejudice against the study of prophecy is gradually giving way before the march of enlightened inquiry. The command of the Saviour is, "Search the Scriptures," John v. 39, and this comprehensive injunction includes the *prophetical*, as truly as the devotional. If the study be not useful, why does the Lord enjoin it, and why did the Saviour reprove the two disciples who were travelling to Emmaus, for being so "slow of heart to believe all that the prophets have spoken?" Luke xxiv. 25. If the fair and candid interpretation of prophecy be not beneficial, why did the Saviour begin "at Moses and all the prophets," and expound "unto them in all the Scriptures the things concerning himself?" Luke xxiv. 27. If it be said, that when ministers and private Christians have as much wisdom and as much self-control as the Saviour, they too may be permitted to expound the prophecies, we reply, that of course no such claim is advanced; but if the true principles of interpretation are revealed in the word of God, as we have endeavored to show in this Essay, then we have a safe guide, and ought to use it. If it be inexpedient to note the signs of the times, and to compare the indications of God's providence with the testimony of his word, why did the Saviour reprove the men of his day for their voluntary blindness? Matt. xvi. 3. Alas, through wilful negligence, they knew not the Lord of glory; and hence, were led to set their seal and sanction to the wickedness of all preceding ages, Matt. xxiii. 35, by crucifying their own Messiah, their God and king! We ask, again, if such expositions be not advisable, why did the Lord, by the prophet Daniel, explain to Nebuchadnezzar the meaning of his dream, concerning a long series of events from his own day to the setting up of the kingdom of Jesus Christ? "There is a God in heaven that revealeth secrets, and maketh known to the king Nebuchadnezzar what shall be in the latter days," Dan. ii. 28, compare verse 45. If a revelation has been made, it is most assuredly our duty to try to understand it, and be wise up to what is written.

But we are not left on this point to mere inference. The Holy Ghost hath expressly declared, not only that "all Scripture is given by inspiration of God," but that it is "PROFITABLE for doctrine, for reproof, for correction, for INSTRUCTION in righteousness; that the man of God may be perfect, thoroughly furnished unto all good works," 2 Tim. iii. 16, 17. God pronounces ALL Scripture to be *profitable* for *instruction*, and other practical purposes—"*all good works.*" Man, on the other hand, says that a part of it, and a large part of it too, is *unprofitable!* I need not ask which is of the highest authority—the wisdom of God, or the opinions of men. See 1 Cor. i. 25, iii. 19. And if all of the sacred volume be useful for *instruction*, then it is the duty of every minister to study the prophetic Scriptures, the symbolic as well as the unsymbolic, and make their exposition a part of his pulpit ministrations. In 2 Pet. i. 19, it is written—"We have also a more sure word of prophecy; whereunto YE DO WELL *that ye take heed*, as unto a light that shineth in a dark place." God declares that we do well to take heed to it. Man, on the other hand, affirms that we have nothing to do with it; that the study of prophecy is useless, and even pernicious; and that to investigate it thoroughly, according to our ability and opportunity, as the command clearly implies, is the mark of extravagance and folly! Now, as if the divine Spirit would expressly put us on our guard against such "enticing words of man's wisdom," 1 Cor. ii. 4, it is declared in the third verse of the first chapter of the last, and what is commonly regarded as the most mysterious book in the Bible—as if there would be a peculiar tendency and disposition to neglect the sublime visions of the Apocalypse—"Blessed is he that readeth, and they that hear the words of this prophecy, and keep those things which are written therein," Rev. i. 3. So far, therefore, from the study being unprofitable, when rightly pursued, a special blessing is pronounced on those who thus engage in it; and, what is more, that blessing was promised and recorded *when the prophecy was* UNFULFILLED. But notwithstanding this plain declaration of the Holy Ghost, to *the utility of studying unfulfilled prophecy*, we are told that it will not repay us for the labor of the investigation, and that, if we touch upon prophecy at all, we ought to confine ourselves to that which has been fulfilled! Nor are such commendations in the inspired volume confined to one or two passages. They are scattered through different portions of the Bible, and reach their culminating point in the last book of God's revelations to the church. In the last chapter of the Apocalypse, as well as in the first, is the blessing pronounced on him "that keepeth the sayings of the prophecy of this book," Rev. xxii. 7. But how can he yield an intelligent obedience to those sayings, unless he knows what they are; and how can he know what they are, unless he applies himself to the Scripture in which they are contained? If our heavenly Father has condescended to give us an explanation of the mysteries of the Bible—as for instance by the angel in Rev. xvii. 7, where it is written, "I will tell thee the mystery"—the least we can do, in grateful return for his kindness, is to study such explanations with diligence, humility, and prayer. Let us direct our energies to the task, and meditate on the thrilling declarations of *the sure word of prophecy*, and our labor, so far from being either useless or irksome, will be a source of the highest pleasure and profit.

The sure word of prophecy! By its heavenly light, in what immeasurable grandeur appears the plan of redemption! Ages upon ages roll by, and still the throng of unnumbered worshippers shout hosannas to the Lamb. True, indeed, during the "little season," Rev. xx. 3, 7–9, in which Satan, after the expiration of the millennium, is loosed from his prison, and goes forth "to deceive the nations," a part of the unglorified inhabitants of the earth revolt from their allegiance, and are destroyed without remedy; yet nevertheless, how vastly must the number of the righteous exceed that of the wicked! There is no intimation in the Scriptures, that even after the three hundred and sixty thousand years are ended, there are no longer to be men in the natural life. On the contrary, it is a legitimate inference, as we have already proved, that through eternal ages, generation after generation will appear on the earth. Innumerable multitudes may thus give full proof of their allegiance, and be rewarded with immortality, as were Enoch and Elijah, without seeing death. And if this be so, with what rapturous transport will the Saviour reflect upon his atoning sacrifice! With what triumphant exultation will he contemplate his victory over Satan and the grave! And with what intense delight will all the saints and angels regard the fulfilment of the prediction—"He shall see of the travail of his soul, and shall be satisfied," Isaiah liii. 11. A monument of the evil of sin will remain in some part of God's dominions—a most impressive warning against all disloyalty—a most powerful motive to persevere in the pathway of honor and truth; but the necessity of upholding the moral government of Jehovah by the execution of legal penalty on incorrigible transgressors, will be so clearly seen, and the will of the righteous so perfectly in accordance with that of their heavenly Father, that the wretchedness in the prison-house of the universe will not detract from their bliss. It is in this respect in the spiritual as it is in the material world. The spots on the surface of the sun are but small when contrasted with the rest of his disk; we can, indeed, discern them, but they do not perceptibly diminish his effulgence when he floods creation with his glorious beams.

The laws of symbolization, which have been treated in this Essay, are clear and intelligible, few in number, remembered without difficulty, and generally obvious in their application. If but a moderate portion of the time and labor which are often devoted to the study of foreign languages and abstruse sciences, were given to the investigation of these principles, they could be easily and thoroughly understood. They are a master key to the different wards of symbolic prophecy; and by rightly applying it, we obtain a vivid and realizing view of the perfections of God, and a more accurate knowledge of his high counsels of love. What was before dark is clothed in light. What was before uninviting, because regarded as unintelligible, is invested with surpassing interest. We are furnished with new and more powerful motives to glorify our Maker, to do good to our fellow men, and to run with patience the race set before us. We are supported under trials, cheered amidst difficulties and discouragements, and go on our way rejoicing. Confiding in God, we ascend the mount of promise, and looking beyond the present scene of trouble and darkness, a prospect more glorious than that which Moses saw from the top of Pisgah, meets our enraptured vision. Surely such a subject demands the attention of Christians in general, and especially of ministers and teachers of the word. Its claims ought not lightly to be disregarded. We are directed to endure hardness as good soldiers. We must not faint by the way; and if it requires diligent study to understand these parts of the sacred word, we must buckle on the harness, and put our shoulder to the wheel. The church has a right to expect it from those to whom she looks for instruction. The providence of God calls for it. The signs of the times demand it. We live in a most wonderful age; and if events, such as those which have been noticed in this Essay, are revealed, and the time of their accomplishment is at hand, we ought to know it ourselves, and proclaim it to others. Let us, therefore, search the oracles of God; let us take his word as a lamp unto our feet, and a light unto our path; and while faithfully performing our duties day by day, instead of being disheartened and cast down by present trials, let us look at the prospect which is beyond, and lift up our heads, knowing that our redemption draweth nigh. The agitations of worldly politics will soon be over, and instead of empires governed by the principles of man's wisdom, and which rise and fall in the fluctuations of human affairs, there will be a kingdom which cannot be moved, a kingdom whose origin was laid in the counsels of eternity, whose manifestation has been foretold by all the prophets since the world began, whose grandeur will surpass our loftiest conceptions, and of whose duration there shall be no end.

THE END.

BOOKS ON THE LAWS OF SYMBOLIZATION AND FIGURATIVE LANGUAGE.

As among those who read the foregoing Essay there may be persons who are not aware of the origin of the laws of which it treats, the discussions respecting them, and the extent to which they have been applied to the interpretation of the symbolic Scriptures, the Publisher gives notice that those who desire it may obtain the requisite information from an Exposition of the Apocalypse, by the Editor of the Theological and Literary Journal, in which they were originally stated, and are applied to the interpretation of the whole series of the symbols of that prophecy; and from the Journal itself, which was established mainly for the purpose, on the one hand, of investigating, demonstrating, and applying them, and on the other, of pointing out the errors of other modes of treating the symbols. They are accordingly presented there, as they are quoted in the Essay, discussed at length, applied to nearly all the symbols of the Old and New Testament, the results unfolded to which they lead, answers given to objections to them, and the most ample evidence furnished that they overturn the current notions which those who spiritualize the prophecies entertain of God's great purposes of mercy towards our race. The principles, also, on which other writers—spiritualists and anti-spiritualists—proceed in their expositions are stated, many of their volumes and essays reviewed, and their defects and errors pointed out.

The laws of Figurative Language also—respecting which as erroneous views prevail as in regard to symbols—are presented in the Journal, and exemplified in the interpretation of much of Isaiah, and many passages from other parts of the Sacred Volume. These laws are as new, and as just, and work as important changes in interpretation, as the Laws of Symbolization.

Besides these discussions, there is also in the Journal a series of articles on the principal philosophical and scientific theories of the period, that touch in a measure the doctrines of theology, and the understanding of which is necessary to the just interpretation of the Scriptures:—such in metaphysics, as the idealistic Atheism of Kant and Coleridge; the Pantheism of Swedenborg, Schleiermacher, Schelling, and Hegel; the schemes of their disciples, Parker, Newman, Bushnell, Park, and Nevin; the development theory of Neander and Schaff; and such in natural science, as the doctrine of modern geologists respecting the age of the world. Those anti-Scriptural systems which have been openly advocated, or in a measure sanctioned and eulogized by most of the periodicals of the day, are thoroughly discussed in the Journal; their principles unfolded so clearly as to be easily understood by the reader, and their antagonism to the Scriptures demonstrated.

Beside these, there is also in the Journal a variety of Essays and Reviews on other topics of interest, as is seen from the following list of the articles of the several volumes:—

CONTENTS OF VOL. I.

NO. I.

NO. II.

NO. III.

CONTENTS OF VOL. II.

CONTENTS OF VOL. III.

CONTENTS OF VOL. IV.

NO. I.

NO. II.

NO. III.

NO. IV.

CONTENTS OF VOL. V.

NO. I.

NO. II.

NO. III.

NO. IV.

CONTENTS OF VOL. VI.

NO. I.

NO. II.

NO. III.

NO. IV.

www.ingramcontent.com/pod-product-compliance
Lightning Source LLC
LaVergne TN
LVHW011210110826
845150LV00006B/1390

9781425517830